Dorsett, Tony

Running tough

$17.95

DATE			

RUNNING TOUGH

MEMOIRS OF A

FOOTBALL MAVERICK

RUNNING
TOUGH

MEMOIRS OF A
FOOTBALL MAVERICK

TONY DORSETT
AND HARVEY FROMMER

DOUBLEDAY
NEW YORK LONDON TORONTO SIDNEY AUCKLAND

PUBLISHED BY DOUBLEDAY

a division of Bantam Doubleday Dell Publishing Group, Inc.
666 Fifth Avenue, New York, NY 10103

DOUBLEDAY and the portrayal of an anchor with a dolphin
are trademarks of Doubleday, a division of
Bantam Doubleday Dell Publishing Group, Inc.

Library of Congress Cataloging-in-Publication Data

Dorsett, Tony.
    Running tough: the autobiography of Tony Dorsett / Tony
Dorsett and Harvey Frommer.—1st ed.
        p. cm.
    1. Dorsett, Tony.   2. Football players—United States—
Biography. 3. Running backs (Football) 4. Dallas Cowboys
(Football team)
I. Frommer, Harvey. II. Title.
GV939.D67A3 1989
796.332′092—dc20
    [B]   89-32122
                                                              CIP

ISBN 0-385-26248-5

Designed by Bonni Leon

FIRST EDITION
BG

To the memory of my father for playing such an integral part in my life, teaching me right from wrong, teaching me things about life that I could never have learned in the classroom.

To my mother for being such an inspiration, for being someone I could always call upon with my problems, for always being there to listen and give me the best advice.

To the fans at Hopewell High School, the University of Pittsburgh, Dallas, and Denver, as well as all around the nation—you were the people I wanted to go out and entertain. You were motivating factors in my success as an athlete.

To my son, Anthony Jr., for understanding our situation and being a well-rounded young man.

ACKNOWLEDGMENTS

Many people helped with this project, and I want to thank them for giving talent, time, materials, memories, perceptions.

My mother, Myrtle Dorsett, and other members of my family plus my old coaches Butch Ross and Johnny Majors were invaluable in calling back another time and another place.

Mikes Bires of the *Beaver County Times* and the people at the University of Pittsburgh—Dean Billik, Larry Eldridge, Linda Venzon, and especially Bea Schwartz—helped a great deal.

Agents Werner Scott of Advantage Marketing, Clyde Taylor of Curtis Brown, and attorney David Caudil expedited the entire project. Editor David Gernert of Doubleday gave much skillful coaching. Scott Ferguson of Doubleday was a steady hand throughout. Roger Staubach, Tom Landry, and Joe Browne of the NFL provided background material. The Dallas Cowboys, the Denver Broncos, Tosh's Hacienda and the Brown Palace Hotel in Denver, Pamela Macintosh, and Fred Traiger supplied information and hospitality.

Myrna Frommer was a top asset because of her research, organizing, and editing.

Harvey Frommer, a talented writer and a guy who is always "running tough" in his own field, did a great job.

—Tony Dorsett

I'm me. I can't just put on airs. I'm not a phony.
I know the way I am hurts me more times than
it helps. But sometimes it's all tied up with my
integrity, and my integrity is the last thing I'm
going to let you take from me.

Tony Dorsett

CONTENTS

PROLOGUE   xiii
I   "A SKINNY LITTLE KID FROM
        ALIQUIPPA"   3
II   PITT   20
III   WELCOME TO DALLAS   43
IV   AMERICA'S TEAM   72
V   SILVER AND BLUE   98
VI   JOLTS   129
VII   GOODBYE, DALLAS   162
VIII HELLO, DENVER   179
IX   OVERTIME   194
EPILOGUE   220
POSTSCRIPT   224

P R O L O G U E

I owe almost everything in life to football. I enjoy going out and competing against the best, and in professional football, you have nothing but the best. I like being in front of crowds, going through the metamorphosis of getting into the uniform, being part of the team, putting on the game face.

If I had done anything else with my life, I don't know if I could have excelled as I have with football. I'd like to think that I could have, but I don't know. Football, though, is something that, once I got into it, I always loved doing. When you love something, you do it well.

There's an awful lot I love about football. I love the crowds, I love performing, I love excelling, and believe it or not, I love being out there and mixing it up—the physicalness that comes with playing football.

I love the team concept of the game, the team working and hitting on all cylinders. I like to be involved in big plays and scoring touchdowns and running for a lot of yards, and all those kinds of things.

I love the smell of the leather of the ball, the roar of the crowds, the sounds of players breathing, talking, shouting, hitting, the look of an empty football field and the spectacle of a jammed stadium.

I love competing, being competitive. It's a way to get out there and take your aggression out on somebody legally. On the other hand, I also love the thrill of not getting hit, not taking the head-on licks as often as some of the guys, negotiating around opponents. It's exhilarating to get out of the way and make them miss.

I love the challenge of the game. I have a lot of respect for my opponents. I fear the licks that people are capable of putting on me at any given time. I see it happen. And it's a challenge not to let that happen to me.

I love the image of Tony Dorsett at the top of his game
. . . king of the hill—set deep in the backfield, the ball
tossed to me, the springing forward on tiptoe like a ballet
dancer, the feel of things, the read of the defense. Then
the slice outside, my eyes bulging and taking everything
in, the moving into heavy traffic . . . the fake, the stutter
step, the spin, and like a butterfly—the taking off . . .

RUNNING TOUGH

MEMOIRS OF A

FOOTBALL MAVERICK

I
ALIQUIPPA

I WAS BORN ON APRIL 7, 1954, TO WES AND MYRTLE Dorsett, the next-to-the-youngest of seven children. My sister Juanita was the oldest, next came Melvin, Ernie, Tyrone, Keith, and me in that order, and my sister Sheree is the youngest. Except for the two oldest, we were born in the steel-mill town of Aliquippa, Pennsylvania. I recently learned that Aliquippa was named for an Indian queen who was a good friend of George Washington's and that a lot went on in the area during the French and Indian War. But to me, Aliquippa was just the hill country outside of Pittsburgh where I was raised. Most of my family still lives around there.

My parents are originally from North Carolina, but they came up to Aliquippa during World War II for the work. There were plenty of jobs available then in the steel mill as part of the war effort. I don't know how much my mother liked being there at first. She still talks about how cold she thought it was when they moved up North in February 1944.

"There was snow up to your knees all the time," she says, "and it was like we never saw the sun." But her parents had come up too because there was plenty of work. And they all stayed on.

Ours was a pretty typical black family. My mom was

the matriarch, the stronghold. I can still see her in her organized way keeping the house clean, doing all the cooking, handling all the domestic responsibilities. I can still hear her asking about how we all were doing in school, giving us schedules for chores, talking to us about so many things.

I was pretty much attached to her and considered myself a mama's boy. I guess I still do. It must have taken a lot out of her to care for the kids, feed and clothe them, and keep a roof over their heads. But my mom never complained. In fact, she always said it was a joy raising her family.

The church shaped my life in those early years. We were all raised in the Methodist denomination and went to Sunday school, Bible school. Religion was always an important part of our family life.

Some have reported that I grew up in the slums of Aliquippa. But that's very far from the truth. I did live in the projects—that is, in government housing. But they were nice, well-kept two-story houses located on the side of a hill in what was called Plan 11. Aliquippa was divided into twelve sections called Plans, where different ethnic groups lived. They were formed gradually as various kinds of people moved into the region to work in the steel mill. When I was a kid, Plan 11 was Italian and black. We lived on one side of the hill, and the Italian families lived on the other. But aside from our not having our own private house, I never felt I lacked anything. My mom would take us down into Pittsburgh to buy our clothes, and we were always dressed in the finest stuff. Many a time I'd go to some of the white kids' homes and I'd see that our furniture was much better than theirs.

All us kids in my family were closer to my mom than my dad because he worked all the time. But I had a good relationship with him. He called me "Hawk" because of my big eyes. My father was a big man. At least I thought he was a big man looking at him as a kid looks at his father. About six feet tall, heavyset, powerfully built, he put a fear in me that probably kept me in line more than anything else.

There were a lot of bad things out there in Aliquippa for kids—gangs, drinking, messing around. All my brothers got in trouble and would be out late drinking. And I guess my mom and dad decided I would be the one they wouldn't let get into that. If my dad said to be home at such and such a time, I was home. I wasn't a minute late. I just didn't want him to have an excuse to get hold of me. I wasn't messing around out there because I'd seen him whup my brothers, and I didn't want that happening to me. All us Dorsett kids had the reputation of being fast runners, but we used to say we had to run fast in order to outrace our dad. He'd come after us with a switch, and we'd take off.

The funny thing is that he moved real slow. They'd call him "Slo Mo." I guess I took after him in a way. My mom says when I was a kid I used to move so slow she called me "Turtle." And even when I was playing football, folks told me that walking slowly onto the field I looked just like my father.

My father had the reputation of being a happy man. People tell me they remember him always having a big smile on his face. But he had a hard life. Working in the steel mill wasn't easy. Dad worked for the J & L Steel Mill for thirty years driving heavy equipment around the oxygen furnace area. Not that that was unusual. Almost everyone in Aliquippa worked in the steel mill. The mill was a way of life there back then.

It was a rough, tough environment with hard and dangerous work. You'd kiss your wife goodbye in the morning never knowing whether you'd come home alive.

There were plenty of accidents. People lost eyes, joints, limbs. It was a real loud place, and years down the road, people developed hearing problems.

And it was filthy. Being anywhere in that steel mill was dirty work, and all of Aliquippa picked up the soot. Plenty of times you couldn't open up the windows, there'd be so much of it flying around. Still, it was a living.

You wouldn't recognize Aliquippa today. The mill closed about five years ago, and 14,000 people were put out of work. Now Aliquippa is nice and clean, but it's like a ghost town.

My dad hoped I wouldn't end up working in the mill. He always told me, "The mill is not a place you want to go to. Do something better, son. At the mill you go in, but you never know if you'll come out." Dad never went to school, but he taught me a lot. And I took his words to heart.

Once I was sent down to the mill to get the keys to Dad's car. I was waiting at the gate when I saw this guy come walking toward me. He was filthy, covered with dust and a mask of grime, and it wasn't until he was right before me that I recognized him—it was my own father.

I was a quiet kid, never talking much. Sometimes my mom would complain that she'd talk to me and I'd listen but not say anything. When my sister Sheree followed me into junior high, the principal told my mother that Sheree talked more in one month than I did in three years. So, as I didn't talk about it, my family didn't really know how I felt about the mill. But I had made up my mind early on that I didn't want to end up working there. In fact, I was one of the few kids from that region who never worked at the mill, not even for a summer job.

Still, the mill is in me. That rough environment, not only Aliquippa but the whole Beaver Valley area of western Pennsylvania, is, in a way, tied up with football. The steel mills were a way of life, and football was a way of life. More than half the guys on the high school football teams had fathers who worked in the mills. Town life revolved around football. Whenever there was a game between local schools—Aliquippa High, Hopewell High, Beaver Falls High—the rivalries would be debated by the parents in the mills the whole week up until the game. Steel-mill talk was football talk.

Also football was the way out of the mill life. It was the way to go to college, to have a chance to do something else. That's probably why there are so many football programs, from the Midgets on up to the junior and senior high school leagues. Joe Namath comes from the region, and so does Mike Ditka. Football is like steel-mill work: rough and hard.

By the time I was in elementary school, football had already become a tradition in the Dorsett family. My older brothers were outstanding junior and senior high school football players. Ernie was called "Speed Disease" because he was so fast. Tyrone was the original "T.D."

I was actually a scared kind of kid, afraid of football, afraid of getting hurt. I remember when I was about ten or eleven, boys would come around calling my little sister Sheree to play football with them, and I'd complain, "Mom, that old girl's out there playing with them boys." It bothered me that they picked her to play with instead of me.

Ernie was ten years older than me, so there was that big span, but he would get after me, saying, "Hey, man, you ain't gonna be anything. Your brothers have got speed, why don't you be like us?" I have to give my brothers credit—they pushed me to get into football. As a kid, I admired professional athletes like Roberto Clemente,

Clyde Frazier, and Kareem Abdul-Jabbar (who was Lew
Alcindor then), and my all-time favorite, Muhammad Ali.
But I had no real sports heroes other than my brothers.

A small number of the kids who lived in the project
area in Aliquippa were bused into the Hopewell School
District, a white area. Back in 1961, Richard "Butch"
Ross, a man who would become an important figure in
my life, began his first year as a history teacher at Hopewell High School. He also signed on as an assistant football coach. Coach Ross is one of those people who influence the lives of so many kids for the better. He's from
Aliquippa, the son of a steelworker, but he broke out of
the mold, went on to college, and became a teacher. Just
about everyone in the Aliquippa-Hopewell area knows
Coach Ross—the kids he taught and coached, their parents, and now even the children of former students.

In 1961, he met my brother Ernie, who was on the football team, and then worked with my other brothers as
they came through the school. So as I was growing up, he
was looking out for me. As he put it: "The name Dorsett
was synonymous with speed, with being a good athlete.
There was a line of progression from Melvin, who was a
track star, to Ernie to Tyrone to Keith, and I was waiting
for Tony. We kept our eyes on the line because we knew
when we had a Dorsett, we had someone who could really run."

But back then, as a little kid, I didn't think I was cut out
for football. I remember distinctly going with my best
buddy, Mike Kimbrough, to try out for an elementary
school team, and we both got rejected because we were
too little and too light. A short time later, though, we tried
out for the Termites, a Midget League team in Aliquippa,
and we made it.

In elementary school I was on a basketball team. Our
coach, a high school teacher, told Coach Ross, "We have

a team down on Johnson Street that has a tremendous group of athletes." From then on, according to Coach Ross, my teammates and I were recognized. So they were kind of waiting for me in junior high, and I made the team right away.

Still, I hung back. By nature, I was shy and introverted, and I was still afraid of contact. Coming home from a game with the Midget Termites, I'd drag my pants in the dirt to make it look to my brothers like I played more than I did.

I remember one incident from around that time, though, that helped make me more aggressive. We played a lot of touch football on the concrete pavement of the streets. One day a kid named Jarret Durham, an outstanding athlete who went on to play basketball at Duquesne University, started taunting me.

"You can't even play the game," he shouted. "You're going to be the sorriest Dorsett of them all."

"No, I won't," I shot back. "I'll prove you wrong."

His comments triggered something in me. It wasn't so much anger as motivation to do well. I think after that I became more focused, more driven to succeed at playing football.

When I was in the ninth grade, my oldest brother, Melvin, died. He was only twenty-seven years old, but he had a heart problem. I was very close to Melvin, who would use his own methods to toughen me up—push me around to get me to fight back, argue with me about this and that. But I knew all the time there was brotherly love behind all he did.

When Melvin died, I almost lost it. I couldn't stay in the house, and I had to move in with my sister for a time. Like I said, I was always a scared kind of kid, afraid of the dark, afraid of dead people. I always slept with a light on. And Melvin's death was something else. I remember that time to this day, how I'd sit on the swings out in the playground, swinging, swinging, thinking for long periods at a stretch.

As a sophomore in Hopewell High School, I got on Coach Ross's football team, and I was moved up to varsity right away. I wasn't the best running back in junior high school. Mike Kimbrough was. We both weighed about 130 pounds. I was put in as a defensive player, an outside linebacker because of my speed. By this time, I realized that I had the speed that my brothers, and my sisters as well, were blessed with. But I was a lazy runner. Once I was talked into running the 50-yard dash. I won it and tied a record—a national high school sprint record. That was the only race I ever ran. I retired from the track right after that. It seemed like a waste of energy.

I remember the first time I touched the football. It was on a kickoff return. I was so afraid of getting hit that I just took off like a rabbit. I ended up running 75 yards for a touchdown. After that, it was a snowball effect. Things began falling into place for me.

By my junior year I had grown some, and Coach Ross decided to give me a shot at running back as well as defensive back. I guess he tapped the source, because from then on I was on my way. I gained over a thousand yards in my junior and senior years, scored 42 touchdowns, and led Hopewell to 9–1 records both years.

I really enjoyed it now, getting into the game, playing on the little high school field in the shadow of the Allegheny Mountains. There were no lights—all the games were played in daylight right after school let out or on Saturday afternoons. There was always a big turnout. Even at a small home game, there would be crowds of 6,000 or 7,000.

A game in my junior year against the Newcastle Hurricanes still stays with me. They were a really tough team, and we were down against them, but we came back. I intercepted a pass and ran it back for a long touchdown. We ended up beating them 21–12. Two years in a row we beat them by that identical score.

The experience of going to Hopewell High helped me tremendously. The neighborhood I grew up in was black, and some of my friends went to Aliquippa High School. Hopewell was predominantly white—of about 1,500 students in the high school, maybe 15 were black. Many of the Aliquippa kids had a hard time dealing with another race. They never intermingled; they didn't know how.

The guys I hung out with from Aliquippa were great athletes with all kinds of natural ability, but they were uncoachable. They liked to do their own thing. Nobody could tell them anything.

Aliquippa may have been a small town, but it was a place where a lot was going on: drugs, babies making babies, crime, deals, anything you wanted. I saw people come to Aliquippa from major cities and get the fear of the place in them. I always said if a person could grow up and survive in Aliquippa, he'd be able to survive anywhere. For me, going to Hopewell High was a lucky break. If I had gone to Aliquippa High, I might have wound up a hoodlum like some of my friends.

Part of the reason I could fit in at Hopewell is that I was never brought up with prejudices. I remember there were some hard times at home, and my mother had trouble keeping up her payments. The bill collectors, who were always white guys, would come to the projects to talk to my mother. She was a strong-willed person with a lot of pride, and it must have been hard for her to explain that she didn't have the money to make a payment. Sometimes they'd get smart-mouthed with her, and she'd tell them where to go. I remember standing there as a little kid and opening up my mouth to those guys too. But my mother always told me not to think of those experiences in racial terms.

Still, I lived in two worlds during my high school years. I played for Hopewell but went home to Aliquippa. School was one environment, and the street was another.

During the week I would be in the pool hall or on the corner, and all the guys would be there talking smack to each other back and forth. It was Aliquippa versus Hopewell, but it was much more than rival towns. It was guys who had grown up together, dudes who lived right across the street from me with different loyalties, different views on life.

A week before a Hopewell-Aliquippa game, we'd be hanging out, and they'd be telling me what they were going to do to me in the game, and I'd be telling them, bragging, boasting back and forth.

What with my growing fast and the experience of playing football, I was no longer the scared little kid I once had been. I was still on the quiet and shy side, but I had become much more aggressive. I had quite a few fights during my high school years. One thing I could not tolerate was when players on other teams dumped on my teammates. To this day I don't tolerate that kind of stuff. You know how kids can be. First it would be words, mean words. Then curses. And then I'd go to my fists. I remember once in my sophomore year I was in the middle of a big fight. Some called it a small riot. I was put on probation from sports for a short time after that.

My coaches were concerned about the quick temper I had developed. One of them, Myron Markovitch, sat me down. "You're like a Dr. Jekyll and Mr. Hyde," he said. "If you don't learn to control that temper of yours, you'll wind up killing somebody someday. You better learn to take charge of your emotions."

Then I overheard some teachers talking about me.

"That kid will turn out to be just like his brothers," one of them said. "The wildness is there now, and the wine will be there later. He's got lots of athletic talent like his brothers and he'll wind up just like them—nowhere."

Hearing that got to me. It motivated me to prove them wrong and to prove myself, to show my stuff.

I showed my stuff on the football field. During my junior year, we played against an all-white school in the area called Butler High. The kids on the team kept jabbing at me, razzing me, and some of the things they were saying were racial slurs. But this time I didn't go to my fists or answer them back. I let my feet answer back. I got the ball at our 25-yard line and ran it in for a touchdown, shaking the ball as I cruised into the end zone.

"Why were you shaking that ball?" Coach Ross asked me as I came off the field.

"I just wanted to show those guys, Coach, that the Hawk is no chicken," I said.

My senior year was a real exciting time. I gained 1,244 yards, scored 23 touchdowns, and led Hopewell to a 9–1 season once again. One particularly satisfying victory was against Sharon High School, which was the only team that beat us the year before. In that defeat, I got hit in the head, and they called a doctor in to examine me at halftime. He thought I had a concussion, and they wouldn't let me play the second half. I was real mad, but my dad came into the locker room, and he told me no way was I going to play in that condition.

I was waiting for Sharon in my senior year to make up for that hit in the head, that loss the year before. I began the game against Sharon by throwing a 29-yard pass on the first play of the game. That surprised a lot of people. Scoring four touchdowns, rushing for a school record of 247 yards, I had myself a time.

But the game that stays with me the most is the final

one of my Hopewell High School career. That game was
against Beaver Falls, a team that had gone unbeaten all
season. It was a big game all right, and I told my buddies
that if I scored, I was going to do my "Elmo Wright." At
that time, Elmo played for the Kansas City Chiefs, and he
used to do a little dance in the end zone.

I did quite a bit of dancing, because I scored three
touchdowns, and the last one went for 64 yards. I rushed
for 189 yards, and we destroyed Beaver Falls 35–0.

It was a great way to end my high school career. I
knew how lucky I had been being bused into Hopewell,
making the team, being given the opportunity to excel on
the football field. I looked up into the cheering crowd,
and I felt like a hero.

People were holding up banners that said "Penn State
—Next Stop!" There had been signs like that at games all
during my senior year. I guess I had made no secret of the
fact that Penn was my first choice. It had been my dream
for some time to play football for Penn State and Coach
Joe Paterno. But by that last game, I had my doubts.

To tell the truth, I gave no serious thought to going to
college at all until the end of my junior year, even though
I was taking a college preparatory course. My brothers
had started college, but they didn't stay long. Keith went
for one semester, Tyrone lasted a year and a half. But
then I began getting letters from college teams and some
college coaches began inquiring about me and coming
over to see me.

Then in my senior year, the recruiting began in earnest.
At first it was exciting. I was just a high school kid, and
getting all that attention was enough to swell your head. I
went around to a lot of schools, and wherever I went I
saw something I liked. After a while, it began to get confusing, and I told Coach Ross, "I want to cut this whole
thing off. I just can't go to see anyone else."

A lot of head coaches came to Hopewell to watch me. This was something new for the school, for until then only assistant coaches had come around. There was a lot of excitement when Frank Bush of Arizona State and Joe Paterno of Penn State visited Hopewell. But I think Woody Hayes of Ohio State made the biggest hit. It turned out he was a history buff, and he spent almost as much time talking history with the faculty as he did watching me play.

I was still a kid, still shy, and trying to size up all those guys who came to see me wasn't easy. I listened carefully to what they had to say, and afterward I'd tell Coach Ross whether I liked them or not.

I got some pretty incredible offers: X dollars for this, X dollars for that. Help do this for my family. Help do that for my girlfriend. I was saying, "Hey, wait a minute, man. How can you do all that for me? There's no way you can give me all those things." But it was serious talk: cars, homes, jobs for members of my family.

One very prominent college football coach—who, incidentally, is still prominent today—approached me with an envelope filled with money.

"This is what you want, kid," he said. "Take it. Come on, there's plenty more where this came from."

I was shocked then, but I realize now that's part of the scene of a blue-chip college prospect.

But there were some who weren't making the big offers, some who thought I was too small to be a major college running back. Ironically, one of those people was Preston Pearson. Five years later I would join Preston on the Dallas Cowboys and take his starting job from him. But back then, he was playing for the Pittsburgh Steelers and scouting for his alma mater, the University of Illinois. After seeing me in action, Preston said I was too small to be a major college running back. I remembered that.

I didn't have much interest in Notre Dame, despite its
great tradition and its many great football teams, because, for one thing, there were no girls at the school. But
I never got the chance to turn them down. Word came
back that the coaches at Notre Dame were saying, "That
Dorsett's just a skinny little kid from Aliquippa. He'll
never make it as a major collegiate running back." I remembered those words too. That phrase "skinny little kid
from Aliquippa" danced around in my head a lot. Oh, did
I remember it.

Maybe because it was common knowledge that I
wanted to go to Penn State, they acted as if they didn't
have to go out of their way to spend time with me or my
parents. Their attitude was like it should have been a
privilege for me to play for Penn State. When I visited
there, Joe Paterno told me I'd have to play defense for at
least a year because he had a great running back in John
Cappelletti. That didn't go over too well with me. I didn't
want to play defense. I wanted to run the ball. Ultimately
Penn State came around to recruit me in earnest. But by
the time they were saying "hello," I was saying "goodbye."

I didn't want to go to a college that was far from home.
I always felt I should be close enough to my family so
that if something went wrong, I would be nearby, able to
get back and help. The University of Pittsburgh was just
about the closest college to Aliquippa, but its football
program was in disarray. The team was always included
in one magazine's list of the worst ten college football
teams. Only about 22,000 people came out to Pitt games—
they weren't drawing worth a damn. And where my
Hopewell High team that season lost only one out of ten
games, Pitt lost ten out of eleven.

From 1964 till 1972, Pitt was at rock bottom, with an
overall record of 28–68–2. Back in 1968, the Panthers were

getting hammered 49–0 at halftime by Notre Dame. As the story goes, the head coach at the time, Dave Hart, asked the referees to keep the clock running so that the bloodshed could end as quickly as possible. There were also rumors that Pitt was going to deemphasize football and drop out of NCAA Division I competition. But the university's president, Wesley Posvar, helped turn things around by hiring Johnny Majors.

I went down to Pitt, saw them play, saw some talent there, and saw that they were missing something. I felt that I could add a dimension to the team and that they had nowhere to go but up. Still, if they hadn't changed coaches, there was no way I would have gone there. That's not to take knocks at the coaches who were there before, but Johnny Majors' coming to Pitt was a big reason for my choice. I knew his record at Iowa State had been outstanding, and I heard he was telling people he had the same plans for Pitt.

Coach Majors saw me play for the first time at the big 33 East-West All-Star Game for players from Pennsylvania in Harrisburg, Pennsylvania. In that game, I took a pitchout and ran to my right but reversed my field when I saw I was outnumbered on the flank.

"It was the damnedest thing," Coach Majors later said. "Here was a high school kid who completely reversed his field and turned a 10-yard loss into a 15- or 20-yard gain. I knew right then that he was something special, that he was the kind of player that I would build the Pitt football program around."

Johnny Majors coached his final game for Iowa State at the Liberty Bowl in Memphis against Georgia Tech on a Monday night in December. At the crack of dawn on Tuesday, he flew to Pittsburgh and held a midmorning press conference announcing he had accepted the head-coach position at Pitt. He received an enthusiastic re-

sponse when he said he was going to have the University
of Pittsburgh football program rise from ashes to the national championship.

That same Tuesday morning, the assistant coach at
Pitt, Foge Fazio, called Butch Ross.

"Have Anthony Dorsett and Ed Williamowski at your
home this afternoon, Butch," he said. "Johnny Majors
wants to come over and meet them."

Coach Ross had us come to his house. His wife put out
a nice spread, and then Johnny Majors arrived.

"Boys," he said, and this was his first statement to us,
"you two are the ones I'm going to build my program at
Pitt around."

Later Coach Ross told me that when he walked into the
kitchen, his wife said, "If I were either of those kids hearing what Johnny Majors said, I'd have signed on the
spot."

I didn't, but after that Coach Majors and his assistant,
Jackie Sherrill, kept coming around. They did a fine job of
recruiting me. As I said, there were lots of coaches after
me that I just didn't trust. I didn't trust their promises,
and I didn't like the way they acted. But Johnny Majors
and Jackie Sherrill were different. Jackie practically lived
on my doorstep. He became real close to my mom and
me. Though Jackie Sherrill was a white coach, I felt I
could relate to him—just as I had to Butch Ross. He understood the black athlete. I didn't trust many people
then, and I still don't, but I had a lot of trust in Jackie.

I think they were afraid that Penn State would come in
at the last minute and sign me, because it seems that as
the deadline got closer, there was someone from Pitt
around all the time. Coach Sherrill would come around a
lot. There was a local doctor named Michael Zermich,
who was on Pitt's Athletic Board, and he was after me.
Jackie Sherrill was at Hopewell High so often that the

principal once suggested that he fill in as a substitute teacher. They even said he slept in his car near my house the night before the signing so he'd be the first one there in the morning. I don't know if that's true or not, but I can vouch for the fact that Jackie was on my doorstep bright and early.

More than a hundred colleges had come around to recruit me, and here I was choosing the runt of the litter. People said I was making one big mistake. I could have gone to colleges where I would be surrounded by great players, where I would have top offensive linemen to block for me. I could have gone to colleges where a winning record and national television exposure would be guaranteed. People couldn't believe I would pass up so many great chances. But I took the word of Johnny Majors and Jackie Sherrill. I believed in them. And I felt it was right when on February 17, 1973, I signed a letter of intent to attend the University of Pittsburgh.

II

PITT

THE CITY OF PITTSBURGH IS ONLY TWENTY-FIVE miles south of Aliquippa, less than an hour's drive, but for a shy kid like me who had hardly ever been away from home and who still considered himself a mama's boy, it was one big journey. The University of Pittsburgh is set right in the heart of the city, so I had actually moved from a small steel-mill town to a major metropolis, and that took some adjusting. But I thought the campus was beautiful with its great stone and brick school buildings set back on broad avenues. Pitt Stadium, built in 1925, was on the top of a hill overlooking the campus, and from places in the stands you could see the forty-two-story Cathedral of Learning, which looked like a shining tower that dominated the whole landscape. The scene was pretty impressive.

Although the Pitt Panther football program hadn't been going very well for some time, it dated all the way back to 1889, so right away I noticed a real feeling of tradition. People still spoke of the eight mythical national championships Pitt had won, of the 1937 championship football team coached by the "Silent Scot," Jock Sutherland, and of Marshall Goldberg, a runner-up in the Heisman Trophy voting.

I reported to Pitt with the other members of the football

team on a muggy mid-August day before the semester began. A few people took a look at me, 157 pounds soaking wet, and I heard the mumbles: "If this is the guy who's going to lead us to the promised land, then we're in trouble."

At our first scrimmage a play was called for me—a sprint tailback draw designed for me to run behind the right guard and cut up the middle. I found a hole, picked my way through it, eluded the linebackers, and then outran the secondary. Going 80 yards, I scored a touchdown on the first play from scrimmage.

All the while, Coach Majors was running along the sidelines right with me, whipping his baseball cap against his body and screaming, "We've got an offense! We've got an offense!"

When the scrimmage ended, one of the defensive coaches was looking downcast. "What's wrong, fella?" Coach Majors asked.

"Coach," he answered, "it's our damn defense. It doesn't look too good. What are we going to do?"

"Don't be discouraged." Majors was smiling. "I think I just saw the best young running back I've ever seen."

Listed on the third team the first day of scrimmages, I was moved on the second day to the second team. By the third day I was on the first team—starting tailback.

I should have been happy, looking forward to the season and my freshman year. But like I said, I was naturally shy, and I found it hard to go out and make friends—even with my own teammates. I was lonely and homesick much of the time.

It was hard to make the transition, to go from high school kid to collegiate football star, to deal with all the changes.

For example, they changed my name. My mother had named me Anthony Drew Dorsett, and that's what I had

been known as all my life. But at Pitt I became *Tony*
Dorsett. I was walking back from lunch during a practice
day in August when Dean Billik, Pitt's Sports Information
Director, asked me to sit on a bench with him for a short
chat.

"You've done great in high school," he said, "and we
have high expectations for you here. Someday you might
be looking at the Heisman Trophy chase."

Then he went on to explain how Joe Theismann's name
had originally been pronounced "Theesmann," but it was
changed in college to rhyme with "Heisman."

"So," Dean Billik continued, "we think it's a good idea
to call you Tony Dorsett—Tony 'T.D.' Dorsett, for 'touchdowns.' It will give you and Pitt more of an identity."

Anthony Davis was playing football for USC at the
time. He was known as "A.D. in the West." And I would
be Tony Dorsett playing for Pitt—"T.D. in the East."

I didn't much like the name change. I wanted to be
Anthony like I had always been. But I figured if it was
going to help Pitt and my game, I would go along with it.
My friends and even my parents started to call me Tony.
But I couldn't get used to it. Up until my junior year, I was
still signing autographs: "Anthony Dorsett."

The way I see it, Tony and Anthony are two different
people. Tony is the football player, the guy who from his
freshman year at Pitt has been living in the fishbowl, getting all the notoriety, all the attention, getting into all the
scrapes. Anthony is just me, the quiet and simple person I
really am, the guy only my family and close friends know
well. There were times I think I could have done without
being Tony, being in the limelight. But that was not to be.

One of my early experiences as Tony Dorsett was dealing with the fuss that was made over my having a child
with someone I wasn't married to. While I was still in
high school, I began going out with a girl named Karen

Casterlow, who had come up from West Virginia to visit her parents and family who lived on Plan 11. Karen got pregnant, and at first we gave some thought to getting married. Then I realized I was much too young and immature to handle that kind of situation. I knew I wasn't ready for it. Our relationship ended, and Karen returned to West Virginia, where the baby, Anthony, was born on September 14, 1973. You could say that was a big day in my life, because it was also the day I played my first game for Pitt. I ran for 103 yards against the nationally ranked Georgia Bulldogs.

Anthony and I have always had a good, close relationship even though I'm not married to his mother, and I never regretted not marrying her. Those kinds of things aren't that unusual, but as I learned very quickly, when you're in the spotlight, it's a different situation altogether.

Even with my success on the football field, there were more than a few times during my freshman year when I was so down that I felt like dropping out of college. The limelight, the demands on me, being a part of everything and at the same time apart from everything—all of those things weighed heavily on me. They took a photo of all the freshmen football players, and the way it came out with me hanging back, separate from everyone else, makes a statement.

I guess my going back and forth from Pittsburgh to Aliquippa so many times during my freshman year also was making a statement. My mom finally asked, "Son, what's the problem? Why don't you stay up at school more?"

"I don't know, Mom," I told her. "I'm not comfortable there being in the fishbowl. I got to be around people that I know and trust."

"Give it time," she said. "Things will mend themselves."

"But, Mom, I'm just not happy. I've been thinking maybe I should quit and come home."

"If you quit, son, you'll break my heart," she said. "But the person you'll hurt the most is yourself. You stay in college. I know things will work out for you."

I didn't quit. Still, I think if it wasn't for the things my mom said and the influence of Johnny Majors and Jackie Sherrill, I would have left Pitt in my freshman year.

Johnny Majors is only 5'10", but he comes across as a big man because of his powerful, outgoing manner. He used to say that as a football coach he was a Vince Lombardi fan. "Lombardi had the two qualities that mean the most in coaching any football team," Coach Majors would tell me. "He was professionally tough, and he was personally emotional. And that's a heck of a combination."

That's how Coach Majors was to me—professionally tough and personally emotional. He was so enthusiastic you'd get carried along with his hopes and his plans for the team. He'd say things like "I want to see guys with fire in their eyes," and that would get to me. They said he could sell anything to anybody, and he sold me on sticking it out.

He was not only a great football coach, he was a great communicator. He knew how to make you feel you weren't just another number. We were allowed to form a squad committee to help make decisions about the team —that kept the line of communication open. The door to Coach Majors' office was always open, and you could go in and talk to him anytime. I did a lot of that, he encouraged and helped me, and I got real close to him and his wife and two kids.

Jackie Sherrill was slow-talking and low-talking, but he was tough. He had come with Majors from Iowa State, and he was a young guy then, only in his twenties. As I said, Jackie understood the black athlete. He'd arrange for us to be taken up to Mount Washington in Pittsburgh, where we'd stay in a high rise and eat soul food. We'd have a couple of beers, relax, and have a good time. But we understood that just as we were treated well off the field, we were expected to work hard on the field, and we did.

Jackie treated players with respect and affection. He'd say, "Coaches don't win football games. Players win games. Coaches don't go out there and line up." He not only talked me into coming to Pitt in the first place, he talked me into staying on during my homesick freshman year.

I ran for 103 yards, as I said, in the first game of my college career against the nationally ranked Georgia Bulldogs. Pitt was a three-touchdown underdog, but we stunned Georgia in that game. They had to kick a field goal in the waning minutes to manage a 10–10 tie. I ran for 365 yards against Northwestern and 211 against Syracuse. Then we came up against Notre Dame.

Going into that game, I remembered what the people there had said about me, that I was too small and too light to play major college football.

In their seven previous games, the Irish defense had allowed an average of just 59 total yards rushing. I more than tripled that figure by myself. Going against their massive defensive line, I carried the ball twenty-nine times and gained 209 yards. It was the most any running back had ever gained in a game against Notre Dame to that point.

Ara Parseghian, the Notre Dame coach, was quoted in the newspapers: "Dorsett's a remarkable football player. I didn't think anybody could make that kind of yardage against us. We contained Anthony Davis, and we didn't

contain Dorsett. That speaks for itself. I think he should
be selected on the All-American team as a freshman."

I was selected as an All-American as a freshman—the
first consensus All-American in forty years. I wound up
with 1,686 yards, shattering the freshman running record
and becoming Pitt's sixth all-time leading career rusher.
Our team record was 6–5–1, and for the first time in eigh-
teen years Pitt was invited to a post-season bowl game—
the Fiesta Bowl. I felt I was growing as a football player,
but better yet, my teammates and I were starting to turn
the Pitt football program around. People were calling it
the "Major Change" in Pitt football, and Coach Majors
was named Coach of the Year.

All of that was great, and as the season ended, I no
longer doubted that I would stay on at Pitt. But I also
realized that things had changed for me, and there no
way I was ever going to be able to go back to being the
shy kid I once was. There was no private life for Tony
Dorsett anymore. Once you become a star athlete you
sort of belong to the public. Reporters and fans would
call me at all hours of the day and night during the football season. I had an unlisted phone number, but I had to
get it changed several times. Being a big man on campus
created a condition where everyone wanted a piece of
me. Just walking down the street became a problem. People would be pulling at me, wanting to talk, wanting autographs, wanting to go out to dinner. Before some games
I'd do a dozen or so interviews, and a lot of guys kept
asking the same questions. It was exhausting, but I grudg-
ingly accepted that as the price you pay for being a star
athlete.

After we had played two or three games in my sophomore year, Coach Majors said he wanted to have a few
minutes for a private meeting. He was never the kind of
coach who spent a lot of time giving a player a whole

bunch of directions. And when he did talk to me it was always in the form of a folksy story, always with a point to it.

"When I was a running back in college in my junior year," Coach Majors began, "my coach called me over and told me something that had a big impact on the way I was doing things. Tony, I'm going to tell you the same things he told me.

"You've got great head and shoulder fakes but you're making too many of them. You're giving guys two or three of those fakes when you only need to give one. You're a great back. Fake once—once will be enough. Then cut yourself loose and run, run."

I followed Coach Majors' advice, but that sophomore year they were waiting for me—I was really paying the price for the success of my freshman year. On the football field I was a marked man and got banged up a lot. I missed one game after getting speared in the back. And because I played hurt a lot that year, I didn't get over the 1,000-yard mark in rushing until my final carry of the season.

Teams used a lot of gimmicks to try to stop me. Players double- and triple-teamed me. I was gang-tackled, teased and taunted. They scratched and clawed, and a couple of guys even tried to bite me. Guys would try to poke their fingers in my eyes and some succeeded. But I came to play every Saturday—against the special defenses, against the hostile crowds, against the standards of excellence I set for myself.

I wore tear-away jerseys, and there was always an equipment manager around on the sidelines with our team who kept a box of them handy. Opponents would scratch and rip away at my jersey, and when I'd get to the sidelines I'd take off the torn one and put on a new one. The manager used to throw the ripped jerseys into the stands for the fans, and as with Dwight Gooden's strikeouts, the fans used to count how many jerseys I would use up during the course of a game. Those jerseys would get mangled, ripped, shredded, but I kept running tough.

But they got in quite a few good shots at me in my sophomore year. After one of our games I went over to the Pitt team physician, and he noticed that I was limping.

"What's wrong, Tony?" he asked.

"I got hurt in the first quarter."

"But you scored three touchdowns after that."

"Yes, sir."

"How'd you manage that?"

"Well, it doesn't hurt me when I run."

Nothing hurt me when I ran. To be in there holding the football, to get out there in the open field, to see the looks on the faces of guys trying to knock me down, to stop me —that was what it was all about. That was what got me up.

We had a play we called "Trailer Ice." Oh, how I loved that play. Our whole offense would act like it was sweeping wide. I would delay for a three count, then go into the middle and try to get the linebacker one-on-one. When that happened—it was all over. I'd fake, just once, and then I'd turn on the speed.

Running the football for the Pitt Panthers, piling up all that yardage, that was exciting, especially against teams that taunted and teased. At times, I admit, I did hot-dog it, and sometimes I paid the price.

In a game against William and Mary, I was going in for a touchdown and back-pedaled the last few yards. That was the way Johnny Rodgers used to do it. A William and Mary player didn't like what I was doing and he banged me out of the end zone with a crushing tackle. It was a hellacious shot.

In a game against Army those guys were on my case right from the first minute. On a 51-yard pass play I was going in to score a touchdown when I stopped short of the end zone. I held the ball out to their defenders and taunted them. Then I scored the TD and lobbed the ball back to the Army players. They came charging at me like they were ready to kill.

Against West Virginia in the fourth quarter I was run out of bounds, and a late hit was put on me. I usually controlled myself in those types of situations, but that time I came up swinging. That got me ejected from the game. Most of the time I just tried to stay in the flow of the game. But it was always a war out there, and I was the one the other teams were trying to destroy. Sometimes you just had to fight back.

Throughout my four years at Pitt most of my memorable times were on the football field. There was plenty of struggle and strife. But one of the most touching experiences for me took place away from the football field. That was coming into contact with a twelve-year-old kid named Jacques LaBelle. His father was a U.S. Steel executive and Jacques had moved with his family to Pittsburgh in 1972.

It turned out that Jacques had bone cancer in his right leg. Dr. Jim McMaster, the University of Pittsburgh football team physician, who knew a lot about the treatment of that disease, was called in to amputate Jacques' right leg.

Dr. McMaster thought it would be good for the boy to meet some football players, and I visited Jacques in Pittsburgh's Children's Hospital, one of five hospitals on the Pitt campus. He smiled when I came into his room and

raised up out of bed and wanted to talk football. We hit it
off right from the start.

Jacques and I talked football, but I also told him about
a friend of mine, an older fellow. "You know, Jacques," I
said, "my friend had bone cancer and lost his leg too. Yet
it didn't stop him from doing a lot of things he wanted to
do, living the life he wanted.

"There's too much to life to give up on it," I continued.
"My friend went to college and is raising a family. He's
making it. You'll make it too."

"I hope so." Jacques managed a little smile.

"I know so," I told him.

I really didn't know so. In fact, I was told that kids like
Jacques, kids with that kind of condition, eventually
passed away. All my life I've always liked kids, and I
especially liked Jacques. It was real touching to see a
twelve-year-old be so accepting of what had happened to
him. I knew I lifted his spirits, but Jacques did something
to the inside of me.

When Jacques was released from the hospital he
would come around to all the Pitt home games, and when
the games were over, he would come down to the locker
room to talk to me. We became buddies, close.

But it was a pitiful thing to see him going around on
crutches wearing blue jeans with his pant leg pinned up
above the knee where his leg used to be.

Here we were, all young and healthy football players,
full of life, running around, and here was this boy, whom
I called "Ol' Jacques"—I just loved the sound of the
French—hobbling about like some wounded bird. It was
the kind of thing that made you realize how much we all
take our health for granted. It's a privilege to be able to
walk around on your two feet every day, God willing
nothing is wrong with you.

My relationship with Jacques, my caring about him, all

of that was for no other reason than to let him draw strength from me. Doing that gave me a high. I've never gotten much publicity for what some might call my "good deeds." But I have never done them for publicity. I've just done them because they have been the right thing to do.

I don't want a pat on the back for the things I've done that nobody knows about. I've been in football stadiums with only a jersey on when it's been as cold as shit, freezing my butt off, doing things for kids. I've given my time, lent my name, donated my money to almost every charity there is. My upbringing taught me to do that. I was told there is a value in giving back. I don't believe that athletes are obligated to do anything for anybody, but I do believe that if the opportunity comes, if there is a need—why not help somebody? If we all did some things to help each other there wouldn't be so much crime and deceit in this world.

I rushed for 1,004 yards in my sophomore year, was an All-American again, and finished thirteenth in the voting for the Heisman. Our team won seven of eleven games, and all the guys could feel something building. Pitt even appeared on national TV for the first time since 1965.

Going into my junior year I weighed 180 pounds, and I knew the extra weight would make me be more durable and help me break tackles that I hadn't broken the previous years.

I was also more mature, more under control than I had ever been before. When I got knocked down at the end of a run I would walk slowly back to the huddle. Then I'd check the scoreboard, the sidelines, look over the whole field. I had always been called "Hawk" because of my big eyes, and now I felt like a hawk surveying the scene and the surroundings, making myself aware of everything that was happening on the field, waiting for my chance to pounce out there.

I had a big day against a tough Syracuse team, breaking open the game in the last few minutes with a 67-yard
run. But against Oklahoma I had the worst day of my
collegiate career. Our whole team had a bad day; we
committed about seven key turnovers and they beat us
badly. Joe Washington of the Sooners got all the running
headlines by rushing for over 200 yards against us. When
the game was over, Coach Majors saw that I was downcast and patted me on the butt. "Young man," he said in
that distinctive voice of his, "your day will come. Your
greatest day is not far away."

The day was November 15, 1975, at Pitt Stadium
against Notre Dame. I gained 303 yards, the most any
player had ever rushed for against the Fighting Irish, and
we beat them 34–20. It was the first victory for a Pitt
football team over Notre Dame in a decade.

I averaged 13 yards a carry in that game, and scored
two touchdowns—one of them on a 71-yard run. That
was on a pitchout where I shook myself loose from a lot
of bodies colliding in a sideline jumble and busted out
into the open field and turned on the jets.

My brother Ernie still remembers the other score. He
was at the game sitting in front of a scout in the stands.
"That Dorsett," he heard the scout say, "can run pretty
good, but his hands ain't no good." Ernie got a little annoyed by that comment and turned around. "You don't
know what you're talking about, man," he complained.

At that moment on the field, on a delay pattern in man-
to-man coverage, I caught a short pass. The second I got
my hands on the ball I knew I was gone and so did the
56,000 people in the stadium. They were on their feet
screaming. I carried the ball 49 yards into the end zone,
splitting the goalposts for the touchdown.

Ernie turned around to continue his discussion with the
scout, but, as Ernie put it, "The cat was gone."

My mother wasn't able to attend that game, but she was watching it on TV and she remembered screaming out, "Go, Tony! Go, Tony! Go, Tony, go! Go! Go! Go!"

I heard people screaming out those words week after week—especially at Pitt Stadium. I was having a great junior year, but I'd pick up the papers and see where Archie Griffin was getting his 100 every week and Joe Washington was breaking them at Oklahoma and Ricky Bell was having an incredible year at USC and I'd say to myself, "Hey, man, you're as good as those dudes, but you're going to have to bust out real soon or they're going to leave you behind."

That personal challenge of being the best, the team thing of helping the Panthers win games, and my own work ethic kept pushing me game after game.

We finished the season at 8–4 and beat Kansas in the Sun Bowl. I was happy about what we had done as a team. I was happy about my individual accomplishments, rushing for 1,554 yards, averaging 140.4 yards a game, and I thought I had a real good shot at winning the Heisman Trophy.

But the Ohio State machinery had been cranking out stuff all year long about Archie Griffin, and he won the Heisman Trophy again, becoming the only double winner ever.

"It's not too many times you get to win the Heisman Trophy," I told the press. "You only get it once in a lifetime—except if you're Archie Griffin." Some people took those remarks to mean that I had something against Archie. I had nothing against him, but I honestly felt that since I had outrushed him in total yards my junior year, and with all the other things I had accomplished, I was more deserving of the award than he was.

That's why going into my senior year I was more determined than ever to win the Heisman. I felt I had a real shot at that trophy. Archie Griffin had rushed for over 5,000 yards in his college career, becoming the first back ever to do that. Reporters asked me what I thought it would take for me to win the Heisman.

"I don't know what it'll take," I told them, "but whatever it takes I'm prepared to do it."

One guy started talking about Archie Griffin and the fact that he finished his career with 5,177 yards.

"How about six thousand yards?"

"What?" The guy was shocked.

"I don't think that's stretching none. I'm serious. I can get six thousand yards."

The reporters looked at me like I was crazy. "Six thousand yards?" They said the words almost in a chorus.

"Yeah, six thousand yards!" It was a Muhammad Ali type of statement, but it's not bragging if you can back it up. And I knew I could back it up.

The first game for Pittsburgh in 1976 was scheduled against Notre Dame in South Bend, Indiana. We hadn't won a game there since 1963. ABC Sports had requested the matchup that early because both teams were expected to compete for the national championship.

There was all the talk about how I had tortured and embarrassed Notre Dame three years running and lots of stuff in the newspapers about how they were not going to let me do it again. Notre Dame had all summer to get ready for me. There was even a report that they were growing the grass high on their field in the hope of slowing me down.

Coach Majors was a good friend of former Notre Dame star Paul Hornung. He was a runner-up to Hornung in the Heisman Trophy voting back in the 1950s. "I'll jump out of the press box," Hornung told Majors, "if Dorsett gets two hundred yards against Notre Dame."

On September 9, 1976, in South Bend, Indiana, in a very

hostile setting, our Pitt football team began its push for the number one ranking in the nation, and I began my drive for the Heisman Trophy.

We kicked off to Notre Dame and they used up about seven minutes in an opening drive, scored a touchdown, and led 7–0. The South Bend crowd was really into it.

They kicked off into our end zone, and we started at our 20. Our first play from scrimmage called for me to go on a simple counterdive with one-two-three blocking. But our right tackle jumped, and we were penalized five yards. Seeing us pinned back there, the crowd went nuts.

Coach Majors called for the same play, a play designed just to give us a little start, a little breathing room. I got the ball, hit the line of scrimmage, bounced off a linebacker, broke outside, cut back a couple of times, saw a crack, and took off with some downfield blocking. When they finally pulled me down I had run some 66 yards. That run took the crowd out of the game and changed the whole momentum of things. We scored a touchdown right after that and led 21–7 at the half.

Going into the last eight minutes of the game, we had a pretty big lead. Coach Majors came over to me. "Tony, we've got plenty of games left on the schedule," he said. "I'm going to take you out now."

I left the game with 181 yards, and that gave "the skinny little kid from Aliquippa" a career total and NCAA record of 754 yards against Notre Dame. I always had a thing about Notre Dame. I could have easily gained over 200 yards in that game, but I guess Coach Majors was truly concerned about his buddy Paul Hornung's threat to jump out of the press box. So you could say my not getting 200 yards probably saved Paul's life.

That senior year saw me transformed from the shy 155-pound freshman into a media-hyped 192-pound senior. I was in the fishbowl. At Pitt, some of my professors made it easy. They even asked me for autographs. But there were others who made it harder for me just because I was Tony Dorsett. I tried to take all of that in stride. I guess I had no other choice.

My phone kept ringing and the interviews were endless. I'd go into places and people would want to give me things. I picked up a lot of stuff—jewelry, jeans, sneakers. Some wondered where I got the money to buy all that stuff. Well, I didn't pay for it—people just gave me things.

Sometimes I even got things with strings attached. A little white-haired guy with thick glasses kept passing out business cards. He said he was a furrier and offered me a raccoon coat. All I had to do was have a few pictures taken in it, wear it around in my travels, and I would be allowed to keep it. I agreed.

The guy brought his photographer in and the picture taking began. "Wait, wait." He kept giving directions to the photographer. "Get in close. Don't snap yet. Get in close!"

I wore the coat. I didn't see anything wrong with that, but the media made a big deal out of it. They thought it was too much for a college senior to be going around dressed in an expensive raccoon coat while the other guys on his team were wearing cloth or something. Hell, fur coat or not, I couldn't hide anywhere. Besides, the coat kept me nice and warm.

On October 23, 1976, our Pittsburgh team took the field against Navy. I had a chance that day to make history. Going into that game, I had 5,026 yards rushing in 904 carries. I needed just 152 more yards to break Archie Griffin's career rushing record.

The game was played before 26,346 at the Navy-Marine Corps Memorial Stadium. The day was clear with the temperature in the fifties and a very light wind blowing.

In my three years at the University of Pittsburgh, we had played three tough games against Navy, winning two of them. That day in 1976, though, we beat up on Navy pretty good. At the half I had 71 yards, and we led Navy 14–0. With 3:37 left in the third quarter, I had gained 94 yards. With my twenty-second carry of the game, I was up to 107 yards rushing.

Then on my next carry I gained 15 yards and became the first player in NCAA history to go over 1,000 yards rushing in four consecutive seasons. We led Navy 24–0 as the third quarter ended. I had gained 116 yards in the game, but I was still chasing Archie Griffin. He was still 36 yards away.

At 14:54 of the fourth quarter I picked up 21 of those yards by scoring my second touchdown of the game. We were now ahead of Navy 31–0.

Coach Majors gathered our offensive first unit around him on the sidelines. "It's so much of a blowout that I'm giving you fellows one more series," he said. "One more series and then I'll be taking you all out of there. Tony's going to have to do it now or he's going to have to wait until we get back to Pittsburgh!"

Back out on the field it was a hell of a thing being in the huddle with the guys. I held hands with my linemen: Broza, Pelusi, Hanuacer, Carroll, Messich. "We're going to do it," they were yelling. "We're going to do this for the Hawk."

We ran a play from the Navy 43 and I got 10 yards. The public-address announcer said, "Dorsett for ten. He is now five yards shy of the all-time career rushing record." The Navy fans were cheering me on. We ran another play. The public-address announcer said, "Dorsett for one. He is now four yards shy of the record."

With me needing just four yards to pass Archie Griffin, Coach Majors called for an option play. The ball was pitched to me. I went wide, cut back against the grain, broke about two or three tackles, and once inside the 10 I knew there was no way I was going to be stopped. I high-stepped my way into the end zone, finishing off the 32-yard run.

Touchdown! That run gave me 5,206 career yards—28 more than Archie Griffin.

I had never been more emotionally high in my life. It felt so good in my heart. I wanted the record, but to get it the way I achieved it was too much. I had said before the game that I didn't want to just bang into the middle and have everybody pile up. I didn't want to just break the record by a couple of yards. I wanted to push it up there so far that no one would be coming along in a year or two and breaking it. I wanted to break the record on a long run with drama, with flair, out in the open with every-body seeing it happen.

And that's exactly what happened.

The fans there gave me a standing ovation. The Navy band played that great music and gave me a 21-gun sa-lute. The cadets paraded me across the field after the game ended. I thought that Annapolis was a real classy place.

My mom and dad were there and came down out of the stands. Hugging my mother, I told her I was the happiest person in the world. She told me she was the happiest person in the world. We both cried, but we both loved it . . . we loved it to death.

A month later we played Penn State under the lights at Three Rivers Stadium in Pittsburgh in a nationally tele-vised game. That was a tearjerker for Pitt fans, a very sentimental moment for me. It was the last time I would play for the Panthers in Pittsburgh.

It was also the last regular season game Johnny Majors would ever coach for the University of Pittsburgh. He

w   l coaching job at his
                                        ie Sherrill, who had
                                        te during my senior
                                        ke over for 1977.

                                        yards against a tough
                                        jors made an adjust-
                                        s into an unbalanced
                                        byed for just ten plays
                                        ck in the I formation,

                                        enn State for the first
                                        gaining 224 yards and
                                        college football history

                                        lled and gave me the
news tha.   n Trophy for being the
outstanding co..._   yer in the nation. I was
the first Pitt player to   award.

Flying to New York City to accept the award and going
to the banquet and all of that was an electric time for me.
I took Coach Ross and his wife along as my guests and
my brothers and sisters and their spouses and my girlfriend. My mom and dad were there with me, and they
were so proud, so touched.

Winning the Heisman is something that I'll always
cherish. It was one of the great highlights of my athletic
career, something I never dreamed I'd be in a position to
accomplish. I set my mind for it, I wanted it very much,
but winning it did not come through my efforts alone. It
took a lot of great effort from my teammates that senior
year and the years before who helped me gain the recognition. Lots of guys deserve a piece of that trophy, but
they only give out one.

When I accepted the Heisman Trophy, I said, "It's been
a long, hard season for me. But this is a very proud mo-

ment of my life. I hope I can go out and live up to the
meaning of this award."

My career at Pitt was the stuff of a storybook—four
time All-American, 55 touchdowns, an average of 5.7
yards per attempt, becoming the first player to have his
jersey retired. All of that was great. But I knew that to
live up to the meaning of that Heisman I would have to
lead Pitt to the national championship.

When we came to Pitt as freshmen, all the players on
the team made a commitment to win that national championship by the time we were seniors.

Ironically, the Georgia Bulldogs, the first team we
played against as freshmen, were all that stood in our
way. We matched up against them in the Sugar Bowl in
New Orleans.

Our team was a bunch of mature guys, and Coach Majors left us alone with no curfew. But the media made hay
out of all that. The headlines in the newspapers said,
"Pitt's Having a Party on Bourbon Street."

We were having a party, but we knew what it would
take to beat Georgia. We were on Bourbon Street at night,
but in the morning we were out there on the field working
our tails off at practice. We wanted the ring.

We took Georgia apart to get it. I rushed for 202 yards
and we kicked the Bulldogs' butt 27–3. It was my last
college game. Before Coach Majors, Jackie Sherrill, all my
teammates, and I arrived on the scene, Pitt was 1–10.
Now we had a 12–0 record. It was a Cinderella story
winning the national championship. It was also a hell of a
way for me to go out.

Endings and beginnings kind of merged together at that
time of my life. Amid all the excitement of finishing up
my college football career, I was already thinking ahead
to the future and pro football. Everybody advised me to
get some representation, so I signed up with an agent

named Mike Trope. I also got a Pittsburgh guy, Nelson Goldberg, to handle commercial and endorsement matters.

As I played in my final games for the University of Pittsburgh, there was nobody hanging out signs reading "Penn State—Next Stop!" as there had been during my high school days. But in my mind there was the thought "Pittsburgh Steelers—Next Stop!" Pittsburgh was where I had made my name and my reputation as a college football player. And Pittsburgh was where I wanted to play my pro ball. That would have been something if it could have been worked out.

I was honored at a banquet in Pittsburgh sponsored by the *Post-Gazette* for winning the Dapper Dan Award as the top football player in the state of Pennsylvania. Dan Rooney, the owner of the Pittsburgh Steelers, was also at the banquet.

"Don't let me go," I kidded with him. "Make me a member of the Pittsburgh Steelers. You won't be sorry." But I knew that my plea had no way of working. Pittsburgh already had a great running game with Franco Harris and guys like him. They didn't need another running back.

The Seattle Seahawks did need a running back. Mike Trope learned that Seattle was very much interested in drafting me. But I had no interest in Seattle. At that time the Seahawks were an inexperienced National Football League expansion team. Just a couple of years old, the Seattle team was nowhere; it had no identity, no tradition. I wanted to go to an established franchise, not to a struggling team.

As part of a negotiating ploy, Mike Trope sent letters to Seattle and issued some statements to the press. The gist of all that was to make it clear to everyone concerned that I was serious in my intentions not to wind up in Seattle. Trope even went one step further and indicated that if I happened to be drafted by the Seahawks, I would consider playing in the Canadian Football League for the Toronto Argonauts.

That was just talk. Canada is too cold; I would never have signed with Toronto. But since Trope was the agent who represented Johnny Rodgers and Anthony Davis and sent them north of the border to play in Canada, I guess there were people out there in Seattle taking Mike at his word.

About a week or so before the National Football League draft took place, I ran into Gil Brandt, the director of player personnel for the Dallas Cowboys, in the lobby of the hotel where the meetings were going on.

"Tony, I know you're concerned about what team you'll end up with," he said. "But if I were you, I wouldn't be too concerned. I'm certain you'll wind up with a damned good team."

III

WELCOME

TO DALLAS

THE DALLAS COWBOYS CAME INTO EXISTENCE IN 1960 when the National Football League expanded. Clint Murchison, a guy who had interests in all kinds of businesses and who some said had enough money to buy the entire NFL at that time, was an excited owner. "I've always been interested in pro football," Murchison said. "I enjoy the game and I wanted to have it here in Dallas."

Murchison hired Tex Schramm as president, Gil Brandt as director of player personnel, and Tom Landry as coach. The NFL didn't give the Cowboys much time to decide on how and who to draft that first season. And it showed. More than two hundred players were on and off the roster in 1960. The Cowboys practiced their football in an old baseball stadium and watched out for rats that ran around in the dressing room.

The Cowboys lost eleven games in 1960, and they didn't win any. The next year they won four games and lost nine and also lost a lot of money.

"Money is like manure," Murchison said. "If you spread it around, it does a lot of good. But if you pile it up in one place, it stinks like hell. We're just spreading it around."

By the end of the 1963 season the Cowboys were still losing, still spreading money around.

In 1963, Clint Murchison called a press conference, and
the rumor was that Tom Landry was going to get the ax
because the Cowboys were losing so many games. Instead Landry wound up with a big vote of confidence
from Murchison and a ten-year contract.

Landry, along with Schramm and Brandt, went in for
innovations. The Cowboys were the first new team in the
NFL in thirty years when they began, so doing things differently was part of the profile.

Research and discovery techniques were used. The
computer was brought in. The Cowboys became the first
team to measure players, to weigh them, to test their IQs.
Scouts were sent to Ethiopia to look at runners, to Yugo-
slavia to check out kickers. Dallas was the first team to
get players out of small black colleges. If a guy was a
good athlete—it didn't matter if he hadn't played football
—the Cowboys checked him out. They went around
drafting the best athletes possible.

Calvin Hill was the number one draft choice of Dallas
in 1969. Calvin was a divinity student at Yale whom some
teams didn't even rank in their top 200 draft-pick pos-
sibilities. Dallas gambled on his making it big. All Calvin
did was win the Rookie of the Year award and become
the first Cowboy to rush for 1,000 yards.

Bob Hayes, the world's fastest human, was passed up
by other teams. The Cowboys drafted him in the seventh
round. All he did was score 35 touchdowns his first three
years in the league. Other Cowboys stars were late picks:
Jethro Pugh was an eleventh-round pick; Walt Garrison
was chosen in the fifth round; Rayfield Wright was a sev-
enth-round draft choice.

Tex Schramm had been the sports editor of the *Austin
Statesman* and the publicity director and then the general
manager of the Los Angeles Rams. He had a way of running an organization, a way with words, and some trou-

ble with players. Once Duane Thomas, one of the best running backs the Cowboys ever had, called Tex "sick, demented, and totally dishonest." Tex shot back: "Well, that's pretty good. He's got two out of the three."

Tom Landry had been an All-Pro defensive back for the New York Giants, then their defensive coordinator. Football was his life and he invented multiple sets, shuttling quarterbacks, the Doomsday Defense, and all kinds of other wrinkles that made the Cowboys unpredictable on both offense and defense.

In 1965, with a rookie crop that included Craig Morton, Jethro Pugh, Bob Hayes, Dan Reeves, and Ralph Neely, and veterans like Walt Garrison and Bob Lilly on the scene, Dallas was ready to turn the corner. In 1966, the Cowboys went 10–3, and they would not have a losing season for the next two decades.

On draft day, I was in my apartment near the University of Pittsburgh. The phone rang. It was Gil Brandt.

"Tony," he said, "I told you you'd end up with a good team in the NFL. We've drafted you. You are now a Dallas Cowboy."

I was as happy as could be. I went down to Pitt Stadium and met with the media, and there was a big commotion. In the middle of all that—the interviewing and picture taking—I was called away. There was another phone call from Texas. It was Gil Brandt again. He told me they wanted me in Dallas right away. They had set up a plane reservation for me at Pitt Airport. I didn't even have a chance to pack anything. I just went down to the airport and got on the plane.

I landed in Dallas, got off the plane, and was met by a crowd of people. I was squinting in the bright Texas sunlight. It was a summer kind of day, and I had just come out of a Pittsburgh winter. I was shuttled around here, there, everywhere. There were so many more reporters than I was used to seeing.

They took me to the Cowboy offices. All that blue and silver was as gleaming as the sun outside. And I met Tom Landry and Tex Schramm—two men who would be such an important part of my professional life for the next dozen years. I posed for pictures with a Cowboy jersey slipped over my shirt. It had No. 33 on the back. That gave me a kick.

To get me, the Cowboys traded their first-round draft pick and three second-round picks to the Seattle Seahawks. The names of the four guys Seattle wound up with still interest football trivia buffs: guard Steve August, tackle Tom Lynch, and linebackers Pete Cronan and Terry Beeson. People would call that trade one of the most one-sided in National Football League history.

Roger Staubach remembered getting the news of the trade this way: "I was out at the practice field, heading toward the locker room, and I heard a news report on the radio. In my gut I felt that with Tony Dorsett being added to the team, we now had the missing piece that we needed.

"Between 1974 and 1977, we were struggling in our running game. Calvin Hill had been our last great running back. Then we had some very good running backs—Preston Pearson, Robert Newhouse, Doug Dennison. I was even running a lot more than I should have. I knew what Tony had accomplished at Pitt, and I looked forward to him becoming part of the Cowboys."

Before I arrived on the scene, Dallas had been in the playoffs ten of the previous eleven seasons. They had won one Super Bowl in that time. But, like Roger Staubach, everyone seemed to feel their running game could be a lot better. In 1976, Doug Dennison was their leading rusher, and all he managed to get was 542 yards.

I liked reading what George Allen, then the head coach of the Washington Redskins, said: "I knew the Cowboys were about as good a football team as you could possibly have. But there wasn't much speed in the backfield. Tony Dorsett gave Dallas a breakaway dimension it had never had."

I also liked hearing Gil Brandt tell reporters: "We realized we were never going to win the big games without a great tailback. Finally, now all the pieces are really set in place. We're going ahead and booking our rooms for the Super Bowl."

Everyone seemed to have high expectations for me, and I was sky-high about heading to Dallas, to a team with all that winning tradition. Coming off my career at Pitt—the Heisman, the national championship—the whole thing was like a dream that became real.

I signed a $1.6 million contract spread over three years that included a $600,000 signing bonus. For anyone that was a lot of money. For a kid coming out of Aliquippa, Pennsylvania, to be getting that much money was mind-blowing. But I went to work on spending it.

One of the things I wanted to do most with some of the money was to use it to get my father to retire. But he would have none of that. He wanted to keep right on working at the steel mill. That work was a way of life for him, something that he felt he had to do. I'm sure that I got my work ethic from him.

I did move my parents out of the projects and into a house, though. But even that took a little doing. We looked at several houses. My mother didn't like the one we finally settled on. But it was a new house, a house no one had ever lived in before. That's what I wanted for them—something brand-new. My mom and dad were the first black family in the neighborhood.

My parents got to love the house just as soon as they settled in, but my mother was a bit uncomfortable at first.

"What are my friends going to think of all this?" she asked. "It's such a lovely place."

"Mother, it's something that none of us have to be concerned about," I said. "If they're your friends, they'll all be happy for you. If not—who cares? If you worry too much about what other people think, you'll only wind up becoming miserable."

In Dallas, I was out there getting my fill of the American dream. Having all that money for the first time in my life made me feel like spending a lot of it, getting my share of the good life.

I bought a motorcycle. I also went out and purchased a dove-gray Continental and personalized it by having "T.D." engraved in burgundy near the handle of each door. A good place to live, high-fashion clothes, some expensive jewelry—I had it all.

Right off the bat some of the spending made people envious and critical of me. Some people also objected to the way I said I wanted my name pronounced. They were going around calling me DOR-sitt, but I preferred Dor-SETT. The name is French, and I liked the sound of it that way. It wasn't as if I had changed my name to some exotic African name. I just wanted it pronounced the way I liked it pronounced.

That whole thing with my name was nothing special, but I'm pretty sure in some way it hurt my image. Here was this young flashy black guy telling people how to say his name. I'm sure there were people muttering, "What's this guy trying to do? Who does he think he is? He must think he is one fancy dude."

A guy like me might have been culture shock to some of the people in Dallas. It was the kind of place where people wore cowboy boots, drove big Cadillac cars, ate chicken-fried steaks, and liked to see their football players keep their place. But coming from the Northeast, I experienced culture shock adjusting to Dallas. Just getting used to southern people, their mentality and their attitudes, took some effort. It was the first time in my life that I was exposed, on a daily basis, to the southern drawl, the slow pace of life, the conservatism, and the overt racism.

Mel Renfro and Rayfield Wright told me that when they first joined the Cowboys, they wanted to live in fashionable North Dallas, but they couldn't. Mel was about to rent an apartment in that area, but when they found out that he was black, the place was suddenly not available.

Those guys wanted to live in North Dallas so they would be closer to the stadium, closer to where they worked. But management told them that there was nothing they could do to help them find a place to live there. So they had to live way out south.

When I first came to Dallas, there were very few black-owned businesses in North Dallas, very few blacks living there. It was a segregated situation. All the blacks were in South Dallas, and all the whites were in North Dallas.

And then there was another thing—in Dallas in the late 1970s, white people didn't seem to have a problem calling you a nigger right to your face. It wasn't that I hadn't been exposed to racial prejudice before in my life, but where I came from, if they took a chance and called you nigger, they'd be fifty yards away and running.

As a young black guy in a fancy car, I'd get stopped by the police more times than I care to remember. I'd be in an elevator with a bunch of white people and they'd move away from me and give me hostile looks. In stores or in restaurants, they wouldn't come out and call me "boy," but the tone of voice they used made it quite clear that that's what they felt like calling me.

But those were small mosquito bites compared to my "celebrated" disco bar incident which took place the first week I was in Dallas.

The whole fiasco began when I came to the front door of the place and was stopped and card-checked. I showed one ID. Then they wanted another. I produced another and then another. After I had shown my third ID, I thought I'd be able to get into the place. But that wasn't the end of it.

The guy at the door told me he didn't like my sunglasses, that it wasn't proper attire. I took them off. I wasn't looking for any trouble. Then I was questioned (maybe "criticized" is a better way to put it) about the way I was dressed. I was steaming over it all.

White people were coming up and walking right through. There I was being subjected to all that shit. Some of those white people were dressed much worse than I was, but that was no problem for them. In they went without anything being said.

When I finally got inside the place, I met a young lady and got out on the floor and danced with her. Then we went to the bar.

"Can I buy you a drink?" I asked.

"No, thanks," she said. "It's ladies' night here, so I can get a drink on the house."

I ordered two drinks, and the bartender fixed them and then started giving me some strange looks.

"Can't you pay for a girl's drink?" he asked. "Do you have to come into a place on ladies' night?"

I ignored him. We ordered a few more drinks, and he served them, all the time mumbling under his breath.

Suddenly he yelled out, "I don't want you to be drinking your drinks here."

The guy was rude, a bully, a loudmouth. I had tried to stay out of trouble, but he was no damn good.

"If you don't want me drinking my drinks here," I snapped out the words in a calm voice, "you're gonna have to physically move me out of here."

At that point he started calling me names that I never thought I'd hear to my face. "You son of a bitch. You damn nigger son of a bitch."

Then he started climbing over the bar and coming at me. I knocked him back into a trash can behind the bar. Then a guy jumped on me from behind and was on my back. I don't know where I got the strength from—maybe from rage.

I tossed the guy off me, and he went sailing through the air about three feet and landed against a wall.

Other people started to get into the middle of it. They surrounded me in the middle of that disco bar dance floor. I knew they didn't want to dance. It was like a scene out of the O.K. Corral.

Oh shit, I was thinking, how the hell am I going to get out of this scene?

Luckily the manager of the place stepped in.

"Let's go outside," he said to me. "Let's go talk about all of this."

"Let's," I said.

Outside we talked a few minutes and then the police arrived. Later I was charged with two counts of simple assault. The charges were dropped. But it was welcome to Dallas.

You could say I had a tough time adjusting to being in Dallas. Hell, I was new in town, young and aggressive, looking to have a good time. But it seemed that every other week there was something—some scrape, some shit, some squabble. Whenever a fight broke out around town, it seemed that I happened to wind up in the middle of it all.

The Cowboy management became concerned. I was
called in to meet with Tex Schramm.

"Do you not like Dallas?" he asked. "Do you not like
being here?"

"Sure," I told him, "I like it fine. But it seems I'm a
victim of circumstance—always in the wrong place at the
wrong time."

Roger Staubach was one of the few people who truly
seemed to understand what it was like for me then. "It's
true Tony caused some of his own problems. But being an
outspoken black man in Dallas wasn't easy then. It made
things worse. He was fighting an uphill battle. If he had
been white, perhaps a lot of what happened would have
been overlooked. Tony got off to a bad start in Dallas. He
created an image that can come back to be a problem.
The way it worked for Tony is that he would overcome
negative publicity, and then another incident would develop and they'd relate it back to a prior incident. He was
never perceived properly by the public."

Another thing I had to adjust to was the lack of inter-
mingling between black and white guys on the Cowboys.
I don't know if it was a conscious thing or not. But it was
strange for me to see it. All through high school and at the
University of Pittsburgh, all the black and white guys
hung around together. We partied like friends. We liked
each other. On the Cowboys there were black and white
cliques.

As I said, being in Dallas was culture shock, but so was
being on the Cowboys. I would come out onto the practice field, a place where I was used to having a good time.
At Pitt, Johnny Majors would tell our team to have fun
and be relaxed out there. He made us see that if we enjoyed what we were doing, we became more productive.
But those players on Dallas—they were dead serious,
tight as drums. Drew Pearson, Harvey Martin, all those

guys. That was all part of the Tom Landry approach to football. It was strictly business.

Tony Hill had starred at Stanford and was a true California type, a loose guy. We were both rookies and became good friends right at the start. We would be joking around with each other on the practice field.

"Man," one of the Dallas veterans would say, "cut that out. This is football, not kindergarten."

"Look, man," I'd say, "this is the practice field. This ain't the game. I don't know what your problem is, but I want to have some fun. Save your game face for the weekend."

It took some work, but we finally loosened up some of those guys. They were conditioned to act like robots, though, and they couldn't change much.

Learning the Tom Landry system was another hurdle to get over. It was something else. The football terminology was completely different from what I had been used to. It took a player away from his basics.

As you're coming up in football as a kid, "even" is to the right, "odd" is to the left. In Dallas, it was the exact opposite. I was going around on the field saying, "Whoa, wait a minute! This stuff is confusing."

There were times in those workouts when I was tired and my concentration lapsed, and I'd find myself going back to my old ways, the ways in which I'd been conditioned. It was a little like a soldier who was told to go "left face" going "right face." But instead of my facing in the wrong direction I'd be running in the wrong direction —that was amusing and embarrassing at the same time.

There was so much to learn about the Dallas Cowboy system—all the formations, the spread, the shotgun, the multiple offenses, all those different plays. Man, it was just mind-boggling!

The way we scrimmaged was also mind-boggling. They

had me out there running behind makeshift lines in a
scrimmage game against the San Diego Chargers. Dan
Reeves, who had a great career with the Cowboys, was
one of the coaches on the scene then.

"Damn, Dan"—I walked over to him—"I'm not used to
putting on the pads and getting all this contact before the
season starts. At Pitt I wouldn't get hit at all from one
season to the next."

"It's different in the NFL." Dan smiled. He always had
a good sense of humor. "It's especially different in Dallas,
Tony."

All that kind of running and contact caused me to hurt
my knee. They brought in one of the physicians the Cowboys used. You could smell alcohol on him from a hundred yards away. He went to work feeling my knee
where I told him it hurt. He was pressing on my knee so
hard that it began to hurt even more.

"Man," I protested, "what the hell you think you're doing?" It was like he didn't even hear me. He kept on
pressing, and I had to knock his hand away to get him to
stop. Later on I ended up reinjuring my knee and missed
the whole pre-season because of that.

Like I said, there was an awful lot about being in Dallas that was mind-boggling. There was all that mystique
and tradition. I thought of myself as just a little kid coming in from the University of Pittsburgh. And there I was
around all that talent that I had heard about and read
about.

Bob Hayes was no longer an active player for the Cowboys, but he was still around, still part of the scene helping out. A real nice guy with a lot of energy, Bob was a
world-class sprinter. His speed revolutionized the way
defenses were set up in football. When he played, no one
could cover Bob man for man, so the zone defense was

invented to try to corral him. But he still did his thing. That was a part of the Dallas legacy.

Then there was this guy quietly helping out the coaches, not saying much. I was curious about him, so I asked him who he was. "Mel's my name," he said, "Mel Renfro." Just from following football I knew his name—starting right cornerback for the Cowboys in Super Bowls V, VI, and X, perennial All-Pro. Mel Renfro was another big part of the Dallas legacy.

Mike Ditka, Robert Newhouse, and Thomas "Hollywood" Henderson were three other powerful personalities who were part of the scene in my early years with the Cowboys. These guys were the kind you would want on your side if you were going to war.

A guy from my hometown of Aliquippa, Mike Ditka was the receiver coach for the Cowboys. He had been a great star at the University of Pittsburgh, had been a tight end for Dallas, and had played in two Super Bowls. Mike was a fierce competitor, one who always took up for his players.

In one game against the Redskins, their strong safety, Ken Houston, slammed an awesome forearm shot at one of our receivers. Mike was furious on the sidelines because he thought that Kenny overdid things out there. Mike and Kenny got into it pretty good, but that time things stopped short of punches being thrown.

In a game in Pittsburgh, one of our receivers was bumped out on the sidelines. One of the Steelers piled on with a late hit. Although a flag was thrown and Pittsburgh was penalized, it didn't calm Mike Ditka down much. He picked up the football and fired it at the head of the guy who had made the late hit. Coach Landry didn't appreciate that show of emotion. But Mike was showing what he was made of and his loyalty to his players. Today that is what makes him such a successful NFL coach, and the Chicago Bears reflect his aggressive style.

Mike Ditka is crazy about winning, and sometimes he gets so carried away that he even yells at guys on national TV. I don't know whether I could have handled that kind of treatment, but I know I could handle Mike's approach to the game—if you don't get the job done, someone else will. He's always pushing his players to perform up to their potential and not make foolish mistakes. Mike brings out the best in his players, and I bet every one of those guys in Chicago loves the heck out of Mike Ditka even though he's embarrassed some of them at times. I like emotional coaches like Mike because I think the way they act inspires their players.

We called Robert Newhouse the "rock 'em, sock 'em Cowboy." That guy was tough. Robert hurt his leg at the start of one season and it bothered the hell out him. He kept taking pain pills and putting all kinds of heat ointments and horse liniments on that leg. It sure smelled up things. Robert played almost half a season that way.

Finally, he couldn't go on and told Coach Landry, "I can't stand the pain. I just can't take it anymore."

They went and X-rayed Robert's leg and found out that he had a cracked bone. Damn, he played all that time with all that pain with that leg screwed up so bad. That's just one of the reasons why I call Robert Newhouse the most hard-nosed modern-day football player I've ever seen.

Robert also had a lively sense of humor. Rod Hill, one of the number one draft choices of Dallas who never panned out, always kept a bald head. One day Robert was waiting for Rod to come into the locker room. When Rod came through the door Robert dumped a bucket of baby powder all over him. That made Rod look like some creature from outer space. We all had a good laugh, except for Rod. He was so covered with all that white stuff that he could hardly see, but still he wanted to fight New-house. Nothing ever came of it, though. It's probably a good thing for Rod that nothing did.

In terms of talent, Thomas "Hollywood" Henderson was probably the best linebacker Dallas ever had. Lots of times he did whatever he wanted to do on the field. He played as the mood suited him—he always played his own game. Thomas would get into the flow, feel out whatever was going to happen, take his chances, and make his move. And most times he was right. Thomas ended up making a lot of big plays and making a big name for himself in the process. A guy with a lot of charisma and showmanship, he was probably one of the best linebackers that I've ever seen. And he was also was one of the best talkers I've ever heard.

Early in my career when Russ Francis was playing for New England, Howard Cosell was building Russ up to be All-World. Thomas didn't like that too much, and all week before we played the Patriots, he was talking about what he was going to do to Francis.

The day of our game against New England, Russ Francis came walking out of the tunnel. Thomas went up to him and pointed his finger. "I'm gonna kick your ass. I'm gonna kick your ass all day long!"

"Thomas, do you realize who you're talking to?" I asked him. "That guy's a big strong dude."

"Yeah, Tony, I know. Don't worry about it, man."

The game was about to start, and I thought to myself: I hope Thomas is ready. First play of the game, Thomas hit Francis with a wicked forearm shot. He did exactly what he said he was going to do. And then all game long he kept dishragging Russ Francis. That was Thomas. He would talk a big game and then go out and back it up.

Thomas liked to have a good time. That was all part of

his makeup. He wasn't a bad-looking guy and he didn't keep bad-looking women around either. As I said, he liked to and knew how to have a good time.

Maybe it sounds naive in light of all that's come out, but I never saw Thomas doing drugs. I never knew Thomas to have a drug problem when he was in Dallas. But as seasons passed by you could sense there was something going on with him. There were some changes in the way he acted, the way he kept his moods under control. But nobody thought those changes were because of a problem with drugs.

I think things that happened to him happened after he got fired. Thomas had a pretty big ego, and for the Cowboys to outright cut him in the middle of the year—that just devastated him. It hurt him a lot and is probably what started him on heavy use of chemical substances. We weren't running buddies or anything, but I just know that being dropped by the Cowboys had a terrible effect on him. Looking for something to fall back on, looking for some escape, I think he just pushed himself deep into that drug habit.

I prefer to remember Thomas as a hyper, fun-loving football player.

Anyone who knew Thomas won't forget him or his powerful personality.

One other guy who was part of the Cowboy scene caught my eye. Kind of thin, he sported an old-fashioned crew cut and wore suits with straight-bottomed pants and cuffs—and that was before they even came back in style. He would walk on the field before the games, and he would come into the locker room after some of our home games. He'd always be shaking players' hands. When he shook mine, I'd shake back. After a time I really started to wonder who he was.

"Man," I asked one of the veterans, "that guy seems to

know everyone. He even smiles at me. Who the hell is he?"

"Don't you know?"

"Would I be asking if I knew?"

"That's the owner, Clint Murchison."

Damn, when I heard that, I was sure surprised. To look at him, you'd never know. But I guess he always took it for granted that we all knew who he was.

Clint Murchison was a real sharp guy who made millions in gas, oil, and real estate. He owned the Dallas Cowboys, but he let the people who knew football run the operation. I thought it was pretty amazing for a guy to invest that kind of money in a team and let someone else have total say and total run of it.

Murchison was great copy for the media. He was once quoted as saying, "I do not offer suggestions to Tom Landry. Furthermore, Landry never makes suggestions as to how I conduct my sixth-grade football team, which, incidentally, is undefeated. We have a professional standoff."

Murchison spread his cash around and especially spread it onto the Cowboys. Other owners lived off their football teams, but Dallas had a "sugar daddy" in Murchison. The team was like an expensive toy for him. Whenever money was needed to make the scene in Dallas better, he supplied it.

I really didn't know Mrs. Landry that well, but I liked her. She was one of the more visible people in Dallas. Coming to the training camp and to all the games, doing things for the players' wives, she was a friendly and classy lady. One thing that I found kind of funny was that she called Tom "Tommy." And as far as I could see, she was the only one who ever had any control over him. Where he was removed and distant, Mrs. Landry was warm and involved with people. Everyone agreed that she was real good for Tom.

All the leaders of the Cowboys were around: Roger Staubach, Ray Renfro, Jethro Pugh. I was in awe of all that talent. But they would come up to me and say, "Tony, it's great to have you on the team. You're the missing link, the ingredient we've needed for the past few years."

I couldn't believe what they were telling me, and I would protest. "Wait a minute," I'd say. "I don't understand that kind of talk. I'm just coming in here to blend in and hopefully help you guys win some ball games."

But I wasn't really helping them win any ball games. I wasn't starting. I was coming in and out of games. Since I was drafted number one, I didn't have to worry about making the team like the other players drafted in the lower rounds. But as a rookie, I knew I wasn't going to be put on top of the depth chart. I knew I had to earn my spot on the team just like every other rookie. But not starting was frustrating.

And to add to that, I could feel the envy and animosity toward me on the part of some of the other players on the Cowboys. I had come in with all that hoopla, all those awards—the Heisman, the Walter Camp. All the top awards it was possible to win, I won. And there was all the publicity about the big contract I had signed, all the talk about the money I was making.

The other running backs who were there—Preston Pearson, Doug Dennison, Robert Newhouse—no doubt, they felt my presence. As a group they even played a little harder. Preston Pearson, in particular, whom I had seen play in Pittsburgh and then in Dallas, really came on and started to play some of his best football. He was probably the best third-down specialist to ever play in this business, and I thought there was no way on God's earth that I would ever unseat him from that role.

Yet I knew that with my running skills, with my talent and speed, I could be more productive than Preston could be at that stage of his career. But I wasn't more productive because I was cast in the role of a spot player coming off the bench. I rushed only 21 times in the first three games in my rookie year. They wanted me to be like a superman—people were critiquing me like I was involved in the whole game, but I wasn't. Not sure of my role on the Cowboys, I became somewhat nonchalant on the football field.

Off the field I was putting a lot of my excess energy to good use. It was the fast lane and it was fun. I was all over town. There were groupies, all kinds of women, an abundance of women. Dallas, in my opinion, has some of the most beautiful women in the world. And I was taking advantage of the situation.

When you're living the life of a professional athlete, you can get anything you want out of that life. At that time I was young and carefree and fulfilling my ego. I was invited a few times to the Playboy Mansion. Of course, it was a fun place and I had some good times there. People were trying to talk me into going there more often and indulging myself in all the comforts and privileges of the place.

But I didn't spend a lot of time in that scene. We used to have our own parties at my place and at the homes of some of the other guys. If people only knew what went on at those parties—man, it was unbelievable. And those parties, they could hold their own against any, anywhere. So the Mansion was no big deal—it was just a place with a lot of half-dressed Playboy Bunnies.

I got an awful lot of publicity for my off-the-field action—and some of it wasn't all that positive. My confident ways, what some thought was a swagger, all of that got more than a few people ticked off. It seemed that everything concerning me was getting into the newspapers. It was like I was standing out there in a ring, a bullring, in a cage like a freak.

I was moving all over the city, going to different clubs, young and full of spirit, having the time of my life. Yet somehow I had the feeling that wherever I went there was someone watching me.

I'd go to practice and Gil Brandt would come up to me. "Hi, Tony, I hear you were in [such and such place] last night."

"How the hell do you know that?"

Then Gil would smile. "A little birdie told us."

I sure didn't come into Dallas with a negative profile.

I may have had a few fights as a kid, but all kids have some fights. So when the Cowboys drafted me, I'm sure they didn't consider me high-risk. After a while, however, they were probably saying in private, "What the hell did we get here?"

Duane Thomas had been a hell-raiser and had worn No. 33, and now I was wearing the same number. No doubt they thought there was something in the number that made us act the way we did.

But after they became accustomed to me and my spurts, and with all the good things I began doing on the field, they would say, "That's just Tony." But that took a while.

The Cowboy management had a pipeline to everything going on in Dallas. And Tom Landry played some mind games.

We got to talking one day about my going around on my motorcycle. It was a pleasant conversation, and Tom even seemed to be curious about the workings of the motorcycle. Then he told me a story about Ralph Neely, a

Dallas offensive tackle. Ralph had gotten hurt near the
end of the season while riding a bike. He broke his leg.
Tom went out of his way to remind me that Ralph didn't
get any pay for the time the Cowboys were in the playoffs
because he was injured. And Tom then went out of his
way to tell me that if I got hurt riding my bike, the same
scenario would apply to me.

That was Tom. Fortunately, Billy Joe DuPree, a hard-
nosed tight end, and Harvey Martin had prepared me for
him and the way he could act. I have to give those guys
credit for easing me into the whole situation there.

They explained to me how Tom Landry lived, how he
operated on people, the mind games he would play on
guys. There were all the times that Tom could make you
feel great. And there were all the other times when he
would make you think you were nothing. Tom was capable of little verbal jabs, coldness, long looks at you. There
was never any swearing on his part, no four-letter words.
It was all controlled. He would rarely raise his voice—
although there were times I thought he should have.

Tom's way with words, his bearing, carried a mystique
all its own. There were all kinds of stories associated
with it. One that I heard a few times concerned a morning
Tom drove to the team practice field. It was raining like
hell. When Tom pulled over to his reserved parking
space, he saw that it was occupied by a car owned by
rookie linebacker Steve Kiner. Soaking wet but controlled, Tom walked into our locker room. He looked
Kiner in the eye. "I admire a man with courage," Tom
said.

A couple of lines by former Cowboy players regarding
Tom got a laugh, but there was more truth than humor to
them. "If Tom Landry were married to Raquel Welch,"
said Don Meredith, "he'd expect her to cook." Walt Garrison was asked if Tom Landry ever smiled. "How the hell

should I know?" Walt answered. "I only played for Dallas nine years."

As for me, if I hadn't been prepared for Tom Landry's ways by Billy Joe DuPree and Harvey Martin, no doubt I would have had a tough time getting along with him. I might've lost it at the start and gone off the handle and probably wouldn't have ended up staying on the Cowboys.

There were a lot of people who came through Dallas in my time there who were afraid of Tom. Guys would come up to me and say, "Hey, Tony, can you do me a favor? Can you ask Coach Landry about this? Can you find out from Coach Landry about that?"

The winning record, the aura that he had about him, those things made him into a living legend. He was a strict disciplinarian, and he could be intimidating.

His lack of warmth also kept people away. Once we were both in a hurry to get out of Washington and back to Dallas, and we shared a limo going to the airport. He wouldn't do any talking. Then, at the airport while we were waiting to get on the plane, I tried to engage him in conversation. Nothing much happened. His mind was on other things, not on talking. When we got on the plane, I tried once again to talk with him, but he didn't talk back. The most I got back from him were short, straight-to-the-point answers. There was no small talk. So I finally just gave up and went to sleep.

Tom has said, "As head coach I was kind of distant from players for obvious reasons. I never got a chance to show them my personal feelings because I controlled their careers, their success. I always loved the personal thing. After their careers I became real close to them, like Roger Staubach and all the rest. But during their careers they found me a little distant because that's the way I handled the head coaching job."

But not only did Tom Landry not seem to have much of a relationship with his players, he also didn't seem to have much to do with his coaches. There was distance even there. And among the coaches, because Tom was so successful doing what he was doing, there was a fear of challenging him. It was common knowledge that he didn't respect some of the coaches because they were afraid to suggest things to him or criticize any of the moves he made.

You rarely, very rarely, saw anyone challenging him. But I challenged him. On several occasions we'd go one-on-one and I'd look him in the eye.

One of those times during my rookie year turned out to be a turning point in my career. Coach Landry called me into his office and told me how displeased he was with the progress I was making; I explained to him how dissatisfied and bored I was with the manner in which I was being used.

"We've been expecting you to be starting for us," he said. "But the way you've been going, I have my doubts about all that."

"Coach, I had my doubts that I would ever be starting this season," I said. "It's not my favorite thing to do—to come into a game, to come out of a game."

"Well," he said, "if you showed some intensity in practice, some more hard work, it might be different."

"Coach," I told him, "with not starting and not feeling a part of things, I was getting ready to write it off and get ready for training camp next year and try to win me a job."

"That's not the correct attitude," he said. "We have big plans for you right now. But you've got to get more into things."

"Well, I guess," I told him, "what we have is more a problem of miscommunication than anything. I admit I could have applied myself a little more. But if you'd told me in training camp or later on that I would be starting for the Cowboys, I would have busted my butt more."

"It's not too late," he said.

It wasn't too late. After that conversation with Tom I decided I'd run my butt off all the time in practice and show him and the other coaches and players that I meant business.

Through nine games I had 522 yards rushing—just 20 yards less than Doug Dennison had gotten the season before, when he had been the leading rusher for the Cowboys.

In the tenth game of the season, in Pittsburgh, I got my first National Football League start. I was pretty elated about that. And getting the first start of my NFL career in Pittsburgh was also symbolic for me.

Although I was happy for myself, I felt sorry for Preston Pearson, whom I replaced as the starting halfback. He was from Pittsburgh; his wife and kids were back there. But that was the nature of the business—that's what they told me.

I remembered Preston's statement that I looked too small to be a major college running back. And there I was taking his job. To this day I feel a little uncomfortable around Preston. But he is a class guy and never ever showed any animosity toward me—not then, and not to this day. As a matter of fact, his sons and my son have become pretty close. So there's always been something of a connection between us.

On December 4, 1977, in my third start as a Cowboy, in a game against the Philadelphia Eagles at Texas Stadium, I rushed for a team record of 206 yards, including an 84-yard touchdown. That was one of my career highlights.

Roger Staubach admitted to everyone that he had a terrible game that day. "If it hadn't been for Tony Dorsett we would have lost," he said. "Everyone knew that a couple of years earlier we lost games like that." Roger added, "That game was very important to us as a team because it showed the Cowboys that when the rest of the team was not playing particularly well, we could still win because we had Tony Dorsett as a weapon. That gave us another great dimension on offense."

I was given my chance to go for my slice of the pie and I made the most of it. That Philadelphia game kicked off my afterburners and set me to finishing up the season with a flourish. I became the first Cowboy rookie ever to rush for over 1,000 yards. Averaging almost 5 yards a carry, I caught 29 passes and set Cowboy records for most rushing touchdowns in a season (12) and longest run from scrimmage (84 yards) and most yards rushing in a game (206).

I was pleased with what I had done considering I only started four, five games. Others were pleased too. I won NFL Offensive Rookie of the Year honors.

We moved through the playoffs, where I had four touchdowns in three games. Next was a date with the Denver Broncos in Super Bowl XII at the Louisiana Superdome.

Being back in New Orleans, where just the year before Pitt had won the national championship, was something special. Looking back now, I realize I was too young at the time to appreciate all that happened to me then. Because I had experienced so much glory in college, I kind of expected that to continue. But as the years have gone on, and I've learned more about the game, I realize how many great players not only never make it to the Super Bowl, they never make it to the playoffs.

I was used to all the media attention at the University of Pittsburgh, but nothing that ever took place there could compare with what happened at the Super Bowl. Tom told us, "You've got to make time, give time to the media."

And I was thinking how those reporters kept asking the same questions and were poking around at everything; some of the things they were asking about had nothing to do with football.

"They expect you to give them time," Tom added. "And that's part of the Super Bowl."

It was part of the Super Bowl and you had to live with it, but it was very distracting. Maybe it bothered me more than the other guys. I didn't like it.

What I did like was flying my family down to New Orleans, getting rooms there for them, giving them the opportunity to experience the Super Bowl firsthand. I also had some good times on Bourbon Street. And there were lots of girls hanging around the hotel, and we made sure we took advantage of those opportunities too.

Going into that season, the Denver Broncos had never been in the playoffs, never won a divisional title. Now with a new coach, Red Miller, and a new quarterback, Craig Morton, who had played for Dallas, they posted a 12–2 record. The people in Colorado were excited about the team, but we felt confident we could beat them. The media made a big deal about the matchup of Denver's Orange Crush defense, ranked third in the AFC, pitted against our Doomsday II, ranked first in the NFC.

For me as a rookie, that whole experience was tremendously exciting. The game was played on January 15, 1978, before 75,583 fans and an international television audience of 102,010,000—at that time the largest ever to witness a sporting event.

Right from the opening minutes the tone of the game was set, with Doomsday II—the Harvey Martins, Randy Whites, Ed Joneses—really into it for us. They pressured, pushed, and pounded. They sacked Craig Morton for an

11-yard loss. They flushed him out of the pocket. They forced him to throw a wobbly pass that Randy Hughes picked off at the Broncos' 25.

Five plays later I got my hands on the ball. Coming off the left side on a short run, I charged into the end zone to score the first touchdown of the game—standing up. That gave me a charge.

We had a 13–0 lead at halftime, and the guys were feeling pretty good about things in the locker room. But we were also anxious to put more points on the board. The only negative at that time was that I knew I wouldn't be much of a factor in the second half because I had banged up my knee in the first half.

The first explosive play of the game came at 8:01 in the third quarter. Roger Staubach hit Butch Johnson with a 45-yard pass, and Butch made a spectacular diving catch in the end zone. That put us up 20–3.

Our lead was padded when Robert Newhouse threw a 29-yard pass to Golden Richards off the halfback option midway through the fourth quarter. That made the score 27–10, and that's how the game ended.

That was the first pass Robert had thrown in a game in three years, and he kept telling everyone later, "I had stickum all over my hands. I started licking my fingers in the huddle and wiping them on my towel. I thought it would be tough for me to get the ball off, but it wasn't."

Although I didn't see much action in the second half, I gained 66 yards in that Super Bowl and felt good about helping the Cowboys win. Winning the national championship in New Orleans the year before and winning the Super Bowl, the world championship, in the same city just a year later was another chapter in the storybook career I was having. It was an unbelievable time for me.

Unfortunately, I didn't get a chance to do much celebrating. They put my knee in a splint after the game as a

precaution. Fortunately, the knee injury was nothing serious and didn't turn out to be a problem.

Many people asked Tom Landry why he hadn't given
me a chance to be a starter earlier in the season. "The
starter must beat out the other player clearly," Tom said.
"Not only in my eyes but in the eyes of the other coaches
and the other players." Then Tom added, "But Tony is
now a starter and he will be for a long time here in Dallas."

Gil Brandt had said, "We realized we were never going
to win the big games without a great tailback." Now he
was saying, "Tony Dorsett is the ingredient that made us
champions again."

It was nice to hear the fine things Tom and Gil were
saying about me, nice to have that outstanding rookie
year behind me. Yet I couldn't help thinking of myself in
Dallas the way one reporter put it: "the love-hate back."

Dallas management kept giving me the line about wondering whether or not I wanted to remain in town. There
were a whole lot of incidents: the fight in the bar, my
being stopped in my car with a girl who was found to
have drugs in her purse, a few shouting matches with
crazies, people who would bump into me, call me names,
challenge me to get into a fight. And there were some
other things that didn't get into the press. Cowboy management found out about them anyway—they had the
pipeline.

In all my time in the National Football League, I met
with Commissioner Pete Rozelle only once. That was during my rookie season when the people in charge of the
Cowboys thought my meeting with him would be a good
idea. I traveled to New York City to the NFL offices and
sat down and visited with Pete. The gist of the whole
thing was that he went into a kind of businesslike expla-
nation of the long and prosperous career he saw ahead

for me in the NFL. Then he went into a discussion of the things he felt I should be doing to avoid trouble. And that was the end of that.

I admit that in my rookie season and even after that I sometimes got myself into situations I shouldn't have. Sometimes I also shot from the hip, said some things I shouldn't have said that I really didn't mean. But the players and the people who knew me well—they knew that when those things were said or done, they were never malicious.

I also admit that during those early years in Dallas, I took advantage of that whole situation. When you come from the Northeast and you're young, gifted, and black, and you know you can perform and produce, you also know that if the team you're playing for doesn't want you because of what you are, someone else will take you in a heartbeat. The Cowboys needed me as much as I needed them. But I knew and they knew that I could not be controlled. That gave me a lot of leverage as an athlete and as a person. And I liked having that leverage.

IV

AMERICA'S TEAM

WHEN I FIRST MOVED TO DALLAS, I LIVED IN AN apartment. But after a while, and what with my upbringing in the projects, I decided that I didn't want to live that close to anybody. I bought a house way out in the country, and a couple of guys from Aliquippa came down to live with me—Michael Jackson and Willie Harvey.

It was nice out there, but the one thing that bothered me was that people lived with their doors unlocked and their windows open. I got to talking with my neighbors and they asked me how I liked the area.

"I like it fine," I told them. "But I can't see how you people keep your houses the way you do. I don't care where I'm at. You just can't sleep with your doors and windows unlocked, especially on the East Coast. You don't do those kinds of things back home—it's asking for trouble."

One morning a black neighbor who lived down the road came over. The guy was really upset. "Tony, you'll never believe what happened the other night."

"Take it easy, man," I told him. "You look all right, so it couldn't have been that bad."

"It was bad. Somebody burned a cross in my front yard. It was scary as hell. Aren't you concerned about your place, being a football star and all?"

"Not me."

"Why's that?"

"Because if anybody tries that cross burning on my lawn," I said, "he'll take some bullets with him."

One cold night, I was sitting in the house watching *Monday Night Football* with my two hometown buddies and a couple of guests. It was nice and peaceful, and we were enjoying the game. Then, all of a sudden, all the lights went out. The whole place became pitch black.

Willie Harvey panicked. He started talking about the Charles Manson murders, about witches and ghouls.

"I tell you all," he said, talking very fast, "there's something weird going on. This house is on circuit breakers. I know that. If there's a power failure, the circuit breakers should come back on . . . there's emergency power." Willie fancied himself a handyman who seemed to know all about electricity and that kind of stuff, so everyone was paying attention to him.

"I tell you all," he went on, "something strange is going on. We're all in for a hell of a night."

"Man, cool it, shut up," I said, trying to calm him down.

"Tony, Tony, somebody's out there. I know it. They burned a cross on one lawn. We're a bunch of black guys out here in the Texas countryside, and we're outnumbered."

"Willie, don't you be thinking about that kind of stuff. Don't be talking like that."

But I didn't have much influence on Willie. He was really wound up.

"Where's the gun, Tony?" he shouted. "Where's the damn gun?"

"Back there."

"Tony, Tony, take the candle and go back there and get the gun."

I have always been a little afraid of the dark, and Willie's being over the edge didn't help. "I ain't going to take that candle anywhere to go and get the gun," I told him. "If there is anyone back there, the first thing they're going to shoot at is the light. I'm gonna back myself up and sit right here by the fireplace and be able to see in every direction. If someone does come in, I'm going to see him."

What I said didn't please Willie too much. He kept telling me, "You gotta go. You gotta go."

But I held my ground. We all did. We sat there for a long time with that one candle burning, making shadows, and thinking our own thoughts. Finally, the lights came back by themselves. But it was frightening, especially for someone like myself who has a fear of the dark. Looking back at it now, it seems funny but it wasn't funny then.

That house in the country was the site of quite a few adventures. We always had things going on, especially a lot of parties. I remember one party at that house. There were people everywhere—lots of women, some team-mates, friends. It was a big party. We had cases of beer, wine, liquor—whatever anybody wanted.

There were four bedrooms in the house. And people ended up sleeping together in all of them and in every bathroom, wherever they could find a place, even on the floors. People were out there in the Jacuzzi just partying away. The party went on all through the night, and when morning came I had to leave and go to practice.

One of my brothers was there, sleeping it all off. I woke him up and told him: "There's still a bunch of beautiful women here."

Rubbing his eyes, he looked at me and said: "Man, this is the kind of stuff that people pay to see. You've got to go to the movies to see something like this. All of this stuff is not happening."

"But it is." I smiled. I left the house and went to prac- tice and came back and a lot of people were still there hanging around. My house looked like it had been hit by a tornado, but it was well worth it. A *very* good time was had by all.

Talking about that party at my house reminds me of my rookie year in Dallas. There was this guy called "Big Louie" who lived up in the hills in California. Some of the other players had told me about the orgies and things going on up there, with all these beautiful women from all over the world. Just a rookie, then, I never believed them. I said: "Man, that kind of talk is crazy!"

One day during training camp, I happened to be walking along the beach with Thomas Henderson and Ed Jones. A couple of women came up.

"Hey, I've never seen you," they said to me. "But we've seen you at the parties." They were talking to Thomas and Ed.

"You guys have been to the parties in the hills?" I asked.

"Sure," they answered. "A lot of people go there." To make a long story short—those women liked me, and they took me up there to the place in the hills. It turned out to be better than anything I could have ever imagined. There were all kinds of couples, some guys brought their wives and others brought the wives of other guys. It was swinging times for swingers.

The whole experience turned out to be interesting, *very* interesting for me. That party in the hills still stays with me—as a place where I went through a lot of first-time experiences.

One night I was having a party and we had some beautiful ladies there, and we were having a good time. All of a sudden the doorbell rang. We wondered who could be calling at that hour of the night. I went to answer the door. There was Duane Thomas standing all alone in the darkness. Although I had heard a lot of things about

Duane and had met him a couple of times, we didn't
know each other well enough for him to show up at my
home. So I was a bit shocked to see him and even wondered how he knew where I lived. But I let him in.

Duane looked around the house, chatted a little bit
with me and the ladies, and just as suddenly as he'd
come in, he left. I sometimes think about that surprise
visit and wonder about it. But like I said, that house in
the country attracted all kinds of strange happenings.

As the years have gone by, I've spent more time with
Duane Thomas. My last year in Dallas he was at the
training camp. Duane is a very complex and intelligent
individual. With Jim Brown allegedly having been his ad-
viser, with Duane's lifestyle and all that, with the negative things he said about Tex Schramm and Tom Landry
—he seemed to always be in the middle of a lot of controversy.

Duane's association with the Cowboys ended when he
was cut or quit—you take your choice. People attacked
him for being bigmouthed and doing all that talking. But I
can't fault him for expressing his opinions and letting his
feelings be known.

Living the good life of a country gentleman outside Dallas gave me some chills and thrills, but nothing compared
with a couple of incidents that occurred while I was playing for the Cowboys.

We were getting set one day to play a game in Texas
Stadium against the New Orleans Saints. I was on the
sidelines, minding my own business, working out my
game plan in my head, when Gil Brandt came up to me
with a concerned look on his face. Tagging along beside
Gil were a couple of glum-looking guys dressed in plain
clothes.

"Hi, Gil. What's up, man?"

"Just a little bit of trouble, but nothing we can't handle."

"What kind of trouble, Gil?"

"Tony, you stay around these guys all during the game whenever you come off the field."

"Damn! Gil, what's the matter? Why do I have to do that? What's going on?"

"There's a death threat."

"A death threat? To who?"

"To you, Tony."

"Damn!"

"There may be a sniper lurking around, but don't worry, Tony." Gil gave me that reassuring smile of his. "It happens all the time. The NFL is always getting death threats."

"Yeah, shit! I don't give a damn what the NFL gets. This is not the NFL that's being threatened. This is Tony Dorsett—and getting death threats is *not* something that happens to me all the time. Why the hell did you have to tell me this?"

"We've got it all under control, Tony. Take it easy."

"Gil, it's easy for you to say that you've got it under control and that I should take it easy." I was getting worked up. "But what makes you think they're not going to shoot my black ass when they shot the President of the United States right here in Dallas?"

Gil just stared at me. The two guys with him just stared at me. Then Gil spoke: "I just can't believe you said that."

"Yeah, well, I'm taking the threat very seriously."

"So are we, Tony. These two men will look after you. Good luck in the game."

Talk about super dedication. Thinking back on that incident now, I should have gotten the hell out of the stadium or gone into the locker room or at the very least put on some kind of protective jacket or bulletproof vest. But I didn't do anything but play in the game.

I told some of the guys on the Cowboys about the threat, and they started moving away from me. It was kind of funny, in a way. Every time they moved I moved right with them. It was like a kind of circle. And every time I moved those glum guys in plain clothes moved too.

I made it through the game and was relieved. Then I went into the locker room and took my shower and was standing there naked, and those two big guys were still with me, standing around watching everything I did.

"Men, you guys can leave now," I told them. "I don't need you around anymore."

They didn't answer, and they didn't move.

"You guys can leave now," I repeated.

"Mr. Dorsett, the threat," one of them said, "is for after the game."

"Shit, oh shit!" I was screaming.

The two guys had my car brought around to the players' entrance and made me go out low like a human snake and get into the back seat. "We'll see you home safely," one of them said.

When we were out and driving on the highway, it suddenly dawned on me that anybody could pull up alongside the car and fire a shot right through the window at me. When I shared my thought with the plainclothesmen, one of them said, "It could happen. But it probably won't."

Fortunately, nothing happened, and I put that threat behind me. That was one of the two death threats against me that I actually heard about: the other one took place when we played in the Super Bowl in Miami in my second year.

We were staying in a hotel in Fort Lauderdale. What they did was move me out of my room way up to the top of the hotel with all the coaches and front-office people. They let my roommate, Aaron Kyle, stay alone in the room.

Aaron didn't like that too much. He kept complaining. "What happens if they mistake me for Tony? Then what're you going to do?"

They didn't have to do anything, because nothing happened with that threat either. But it's an awful feeling to hear that someone wants to take a shot at you. Especially in a stadium, where there's no way you can hide from anybody. If there's a guy with a high-powered rifle with a scope on it, you're totally helpless. You can run but you can't hide.

A couple of years ago, in Los Angeles, there was an assassination threat against Coach Landry. He was out there coaching and ignoring the whole thing. You had to admire his courage, but you couldn't believe he was doing that. We were even losing the game, getting beat pretty good. They were telling guys to stand by Tom, to surround him. And guys were saying, "Hey, what if someone takes a shot and misses?"

No one wanted to be too close to Tom. Guys were around him and then you could see they did a little slide to the right, to the left. They tried to wiggle out of firing range.

I guess a lot of us in professional football have had death threats against us—some that we've known about and probably many others that no one informed us of. You have to take those things seriously. There are all kinds of crazy people in this world. The game of football is such a great game, and we all love it. We're just out there competing and not doing anything to harm anybody. I just can't figure out why anyone would want to hurt an athlete. We just play games.

Dallas management played lots of games too. That made being on the Cowboys at times a lot like being in the Brave New World, where gimmicks and control went with the territory.

Punctuality was one of Tom Landry's big things. He was never late for anything, and he had this expression: "You have to plan for disasters." I agreed that players had to be on time for meetings. But there was never any give-and-take at all as far as lateness was concerned, no one ever got the benefit of the doubt. If there was a rainstorm or a snowstorm or some problem with traffic—that didn't matter. If you didn't get to a meeting on time, you'd get fined, regardless of your reason. The next time you were late the fine doubled, then tripled, then quadrupled. Flexibility, human consideration, were never part of the deal.

In my second season with the team I experienced that inflexibility firsthand. My mom and dad had come down to Dallas to watch me play in a game scheduled against the Philadelphia Eagles on October 21, 1978. We had a Saturday practice and I overslept.

"Don't you think you ought to call someone?" my dad asked. "Won't you get into trouble?"

"I don't have anyone to call," I told him. "It's no big deal anyway. It's just a Saturday practice, a little dress rehearsal. We don't do anything much but walk through things."

The next day I got to the stadium and was told that Coach Landry wanted to see me.

"What happened yesterday?" he asked.

"I overslept. Sorry about that."

"That's too bad," he said. "You're not going to start this game and you probably won't even play."

"But, Coach," I protested, really taken aback, "I have to play. My family has come down here. They've come thousands of miles to see me play. This is what my life is all about, my family." Tom just looked at me, not saying anything, so I continued.

"Is it because it's me?" I asked. "Others have done this before, missed a Saturday practice, and they've played. I've got to play. I've got to play." I was pleading with the man, almost begging.

"You won't play," he said softly.

I was so angry. My eyes filled with water. I was hurt. I was hurt real bad. That was a time I wanted to try Tom Landry. I was about ready then to get up and cut across the room and tell him, "Hey, you whip my ass or I whip you." That's how furious I was.

That was Tom and the total control he had. There was no way you could go over his head to Tex Schramm or anybody else. Tom Landry ran that team, period.

I'll never forget that incident. It showed me just how unfeeling Tom Landry could be. I understood discipline, but that was too much. I did get to play late in that game, but the way he handled that situation, he was more like a computer than a human being.

A kind of fetish about punctuality was part of Tom's atmosphere of control, and some silly rules and regulations were also part of the picture. There was a strict rule that no one could wear a baseball cap at meetings. It wasn't like we were sitting in some auditorium where everyone was dressed in black tie. But if guys came to meetings with caps on their heads and they didn't take them off, they'd get fined. That was ridiculous. Wearing a cap doesn't stop anybody from concentrating.

The control mentality of the Dallas system was everywhere. On the road Dallas management would treat us like boys by putting security on the floors of the hotels that we stayed in. No one was allowed on the floor to visit you—they couldn't even get up to one of those

floors. If your mother wanted to visit you, she wasn't allowed up. Players had to go down to the lobby to visit
with any friend or relative who came calling. Man, that
was always an uncomfortable situation, being in the
lobby with all those people, those fans, just hanging
around. Guys complained, but it was just another example of the Cowboy way of life. It was not a free atmosphere.

The atmosphere of control was even extended to the
Dallas Cowgirls. The Cowboys were one of the first
teams to have cheerleaders. And the Cowgirls have
brought a lot of glamour and glitter to Texas Stadium and
added to the image of the team. Some of the Cowgirls
have become extremely famous. They've traveled the
world, been on military bases, gotten parts on TV, had
movie roles. Being a Cowboy cheerleader has truly
helped many girls get discovered and enhanced their
lives, but it's also enhanced the mystique of the Cowboys.

At one time all the Cowgirls were very attractive. In
recent years they haven't been as pretty as some of the
girls who are cheerleaders for other teams around the
league. And there have always been a couple of black
girls scattered in there on the Cowgirls, although not
many.

I've seen lots of black girls try out, and I've also seen
that the Cowboys wouldn't hire the real pretty black
girls. I'm not saying that the black girls they get are ugly,
but I am saying that many times some of the better-look-
ing girls have not been picked. Suzanne Mitchell is in
charge of the whole thing and supposedly does the picking of the Cowgirls. I guess she's got her standards.

But I could never understand why they didn't allow
Cowboy players to date any of the Cowgirls. That was a
silly thing. Other teams in the NFL allow dating. Jim Jen-

Coach Butch Ross, one of my favorite people, at one of his favorite places, the field at Hopewell High. COURTESY BUTCH ROSS

Here I am in Pitt Stadium—workouts, sprints, and
memories.   UNIVERSITY OF PITTSBURGH

Meeting President Gerald Ford was one of the high
points—off the field—of my college career.

UNIVERSITY OF PITTSBURGH

Running to daylight—a thing I loved to do at Pitt.

UNIVERSITY OF PITTSBURGH

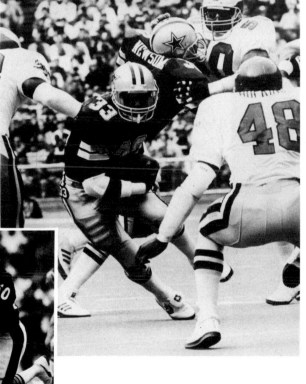

Getting a little help from Timmy Newsome against the Philadelphia Eagles.

THE DALLAS COWBOYS WEEKLY

They called me "bug eyes"—you can see why.

THE DALLAS COWBOYS WEEKLY

Running tough all the way into the end zone.

THE DALLAS COWBOYS WEEKLY

Here I am against what seemed like the entire Steel Curtain—we won that game 27–13.   *THE DALLAS COWBOYS WEEKLY*

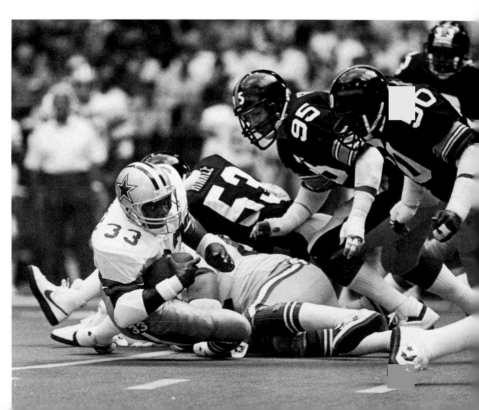

Waiting, waiting for my moment.   *THE DALLAS COWBOYS WEEKLY*

"Captain America" and "TD" taking on the Eagles.
THE DALLAS COWBOYS WEEKLY

Sweating it off and getting it on at training camp.
THE DALLAS COWBOYS WEEKLY

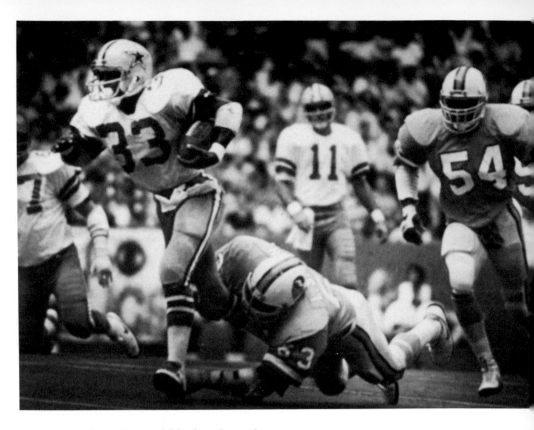

Another inch and I would be breaking this one.

THE DALLAS COWBOYS WEEKLY

Getting set to give my "hello–good-bye" move.

THE DALLAS COWBOYS WEEKLY

Horsing around with
some of my young fans.
THE DALLAS
COWBOYS WEEKLY

Even on the sidelines I was always into the game.
THE DALLAS COWBOYS WEEKLY

A new uniform—Denver—
but the same me!
ERIC LARS BAKKE/
DENVER BRONCOS

Finding a hole in the Kan-
sas City line.
ERIC LARS BAKKE/
DENVER BRONCOS

sen of Miami not only dated one of the Dolphin cheerleaders—he married her.

Over the years some of the players on the Cowboys did
date Cowgirls despite the rule against it. I dated one or
two myself. It was understood that the first time a girl
was caught dating a player she would be fined and sus-
pended. Then if the girl was caught dating a player a
second time, she would be fired. The whole thing was
really pathetic, considering the girls were getting paid
about fifteen dollars a game.

What you had to do if you wanted to date one of the
Cowgirls was to sneak around, do it on the sly, watch out
so that no one would see you together. Damn, it was not
even worth the effort. But that attitude about dating . . .
who you dated . . . what you did with your personal life
. . . that was all part of the Cowboy control package.

Part of the scene in Dallas was interracial dating. You'd
have guys dating interracially just as people do all over
America. But Cowboy management (and everyone else
down there in Dallas) didn't like it. There was not very
much they could do about it, however. I dated white girls.
I had no prejudices even if other people did.

One day a reporter came up to me: "What do you think
Coach Landry thinks about some of the girls you date?"

That kind of question ticked me off. I responded: "Tom
Landry cannot pick and choose who I date. He's only my
coach. He's not my father. He doesn't run my life. I'm a
man just like he is."

I did as I pleased, and I didn't please some people, but
they couldn't change me to fit the system. The Cowboy
control was everywhere—aimed at where you lived, your
social life, who you dated, what kind of friends you had,
what you said and how you said it. The atmosphere had
to affect me, but it couldn't break me. I spoke my mind.

Sometimes, I guess, I could have been maybe a little more tactful, but that was me and is me—I'm my own man.

So many of the things that went on in Dallas were not related to football, just gimmicks to use up our time, to get data and results, and cross-checks for cross-checks. It seemed we had to get involved with anything they could get their hands on that supposedly improved the skills of players.

The whole system was into computers in a big way. I guess they thought that they'd feed all the data and statistics into a computer and it would work away and spit out super football players.

The drills, tests, routines, games, and other stuff we went through at the mini-camps in Dallas—I haven't seen that kind of stuff with other NFL teams. Nobody could understand why we had to go through that crap. What did it all have to do with making us better football players? Guys complained about it, but there wasn't much we could do. Since they were part of the contract, we did them.

They knew what we could do as football players, they'd seen us in action, yet they were always out there calculating. Like they always wanted to see your fastest time in races against other guys. Some players just went through the motions; others did it as a private competition between each other.

Dr. Bob Ward, the Dallas strength and conditioning coach, was high on a thing they called the "sensory deprivation tank." Filled with salt water, the tank had an apparatus you lay down on, something like a tanning bed. You were there in total darkness. You'd lie there enclosed by water. You thought if you got too laid back and fell asleep, you'd drown. But there was so much salt water there that it kept you afloat. Guys said there was more salt in there than the Great Salt Lake.

They claimed that the tank was supposed to enhance your mind's capability and relax you at the same time. It was equipped with audio and visual stimuli. You could listen to tapes, watch a game film, study an opponent, watch yourself on film.

I got in there once—once was enough for me. I wouldn't let them close the door on me. Then when I felt what it was like, I got the hell out of there fast. Man, you could easily get claustrophobia in that thing.

That tank wasn't too popular among the guys; only Rafael Septien, our kicker, loved it. He'd spend hours in there all alone. I don't know what he was doing all the time he was in there. Probably sleeping.

Kickers dance to a different drummer anyway. They're like space cadets because their elevator doesn't go up all the way. A lot of them seem so flaky that you wouldn't think they could withstand the pressure of the big games, all those crucial moments when the game depends so much on what they can do. They run out, kick the ball, go back, and sit on the sidelines until they get called again. They don't have much to do, but they get paid well for it.

Punters as well as place kickers are there every day with the team, but they're also apart from the team. They don't have much to do in practices; they don't burn up a lot of energy like the rest of the players. Those kickers can be out there for just part of a team's practice and then they can go off and do their own thing.

When Rafael Septien was kicking well for Dallas, he was one of the best at his job in the entire league. Sometimes I'd see him reading a book and eating an apple on the sidelines during a game. That used to piss me off. We needed that guy to be ready if the game was close. We needed him to be in the game. But there he was in his own world. Like I said, though, kickers are a different breed.

Another gimmick the Cowboys loved was a computer that lit up and beeped. You had to keep pace with its directions. One of your hands was supposed to do one thing while the other did something else. Then it got more complicated by involving your feet too. One foot pressed and the other did something else. They claimed it was a way of testing and developing coordination—feet and hands working together with the eyes. I thought the whole thing was silly, a waste of time.

We also were made to perform like jumping jacks on different boxes at different heights. You'd jump off one of the boxes and onto the next one and keep up that routine for a while—jump up, down, up, down. They said that stuff was to help your explosiveness as a player. To me, that was also kind of stupid. A couple of guys even blew their knees out doing that nonsense.

Jumping was a big part of the scene—long jumps, triple jumps, all kinds of jumping exercises. And all of it was supervised. You'd go down, run, jump off a disk, and then triple-jump. For what? If I can triple-jump so far, I wondered, that means I can do what on the football field?

With some of the drills they had us do on ropes and monkey bars, I used to wonder whether we were football players or gymnasts. We'd be climbing up these ropes a few times in a row and get timed. And we'd go up and down on monkey bars, swing across the monkey bars. They'd have a stopwatch out to see how fast you could manage that. Guys would be straining, pushing it, hurting their shoulders, messing up their arms.

"What good is this going to do—seeing how fast we can climb monkey bars?" some of the guys asked. "How's all this relate to football?" others wondered.

"It's to develop and measure agility," we were told. At

least we were given a reason, but like I said, to me all of that was a waste of time.

Then there was this sandpit thing. We'd have to do a 30- or 40-yard sprint through this track that was covered with sand. Guys would be moaning, groaning, falling on their faces. And they would ask questions like "Why do we have to run through sand?" "What good is this going to do for us?" "There's not going to be any sand on the field when we play during a game, so why the hell do we have to run through this shit now?"

Maybe the most ridiculous thing we had to do was pull a sled that had resistance on it that was hooked up to a machine. They would time us to see how fast we could run down a track pulling that ungodly weight. One time I was out there pulling like some damn mule, and I was pulling so hard that I hurt my back. Later on I found out that they had put the wrong weight on when they hooked up that damn contraption.

That sled was something else. Guys would blow out their knees or wrench their backs pulling it down the track. You don't ever get out on the field in the NFL and pull somebody. It was all silly.

Guys coming to the Cowboys as rookies couldn't believe what the team went through. Tom Landry would work the hell out of us. Players on other teams couldn't believe how hard we had to work, couldn't understand all those games, gimmicks, toys, and drills Dallas made us get involved with.

There were a couple of drills, though, that I thought did have some football value. One was a course that was dotted with cones and hurdles. You had to swerve and stop, speed up, and turn on a dime to get through it. At least that tested and helped you develop perception and running skills.

The "Agility–Speed–Unexpected Visual Stimulus Test"

was a big thing there. Flashing colored lights—like many different traffic lights—directed the runner in different directions. That, too, had some validity for football. As a runner, you have to change directions. It's color, flashes of color, that gets you to go in different directions once you see somebody coming at you. How long it takes you to react to all that can be the difference between a loss, a one-yard gain, or making 50 yards. They all made a big deal about how no one came close to me in handling that test.

No doubt the Cowboys have excellent training facilities, fine equipment, and a real good strength and conditioning program. It was just that I, and lots of other guys, had some problems with the way they made use of all that.

For one thing there were off-season programs and workouts set up for the players. That was fine. But management used that as a way to keep control of things. They kept attendance records. They encouraged you to live right there in the city. If you didn't live there, they tried to get you to move, explaining that it was in your best interests as far as making the Cowboys or playing for the Cowboys was concerned. It was much more than subtle pressure. And as for those off-season workouts—other National Football League teams are paying guys to give up their time and take part in them. The Cowboys never did, and they probably never will.

I believe in being a fine, well-conditioned athlete, but I also believe in the value of pacing yourself, listening to your own body, adjusting workouts to the needs of the individual. Bob Ward and the others there in charge of all that strength and conditioning had their own ideas. But I knew I had the best read on what was good for my own body. Bob and I used to go back and forth over the same ground—he would be telling me what he thought was good for me and I would be telling him what I wanted to do with my own body.

When I first joined Dallas, they made me lift weights with my legs and my legs started to tighten up. I had more knee problems my rookie year than I had ever had before in my life. I complained that I never believed in squats. Lifting for upper-body strength was something I saw value in, but as far as my legs were concerned, I thought that for me running was the best form of exercise. Other guys went with the flow and did what they were told. I didn't. It took me a little while to convince them, but I finally made my point and they let me do my own thing. All those years in Dallas, I followed my own workout routine most of the time.

I'm a big believer in burnout. And I saw quite a few examples of that on the Dallas Cowboys. I thought we were made to do too much running during the season. Late in the year, when our bodies were weary, our legs were gone, and we were all beat up, they still made us run. It was ridiculous—all that running. They made us get out there and do those 40s, those 110s, those 175s. Man, it was tough!

In the off-season program, Bob Ward had guys do a lot of running leading up to the training camp. They busted their butts. Then there was all that weight lifting: the barbells, dumbbells. It was a controlled situation, and guys were programmed into it, threw themselves into it. A lot of them just followed orders and didn't pace themselves.

It was sad because we had a lot of guys, especially guys who worked real hard, winding up getting injured. They followed the program to the letter, and they paid the price.

Paying the price, playing with pain and injuries, getting screwed around—those things were a big part of the scene there with the Cowboys.

Doug Donley came up with a bad problem with his shoulder at a practice. The guy was really suffering when his shoulder popped out. They took him to the doctor's, which was a block and a half down the street. When they checked him out, they decided that they'd shoot him up, throw the shoulder back in, and send him back to the practice field.

I was amazed to see Doug out there going through his paces after having seen the pain he was in just a short time before. He was out there again, practicing like nothing had happened.

"Man, we don't need you out here on the practice field," I said, concerned about him. "We need you in the game. This is not the way for you to go about things. You should be in there resting and getting treatment on your shoulder. You've got to be taking care of yourself. If you keep doing what you're doing, you'll end your career."

Later on in meetings during the season Tom Landry would come over and start to play psychological games with Doug. "He's playing with a lot of pain." Tom was really pumping him up. "But Doug is courageous. That's what football is all about."

Doug fell for all that praise. He went on to play that season with a lot of pain—you could look at his face and see what he was going through. The season ended and we all went through the off-season and then into the mini-camp. Doug told us how he had busted his butt that off-season strengthening his shoulder. "I really worked at it to get back to where I was before the injury," he said.

In the mini-camp we always did a lot of dips, and Doug was doing more dips than I had ever seen him do before. It looked to everyone that his shoulder was much stronger.

The mini-camp came to an end, and Tom called Doug in for a talk. The gist of it was that Tom told Doug that he was no longer part of the Cowboys' plans and that he was going to be released. Doug also learned that the Cowboys knew when the last season had ended that they had no use for him, that he didn't figure in the team's future. It was another example of how a guy got screwed by the Cowboys, and it upset the hell out of Doug.

"Why, Coach," he asked, "if you knew you didn't have any use for me, why did I have to go through a whole off-season busting my butt, go through the mini-camp knocking myself out? Why didn't somebody tell me?"

Tom's answer: "There was a communications problem."

Another way Tom Landry could play mind games was shown in how he treated Timmy Newsome. A big, strong guy with a lot of talent, Timmy could've had an illustrious career if he had played for some team other than Dallas. With the Cowboys there were flashes of greatness, but Timmy was never put in a position where he could show off his talent. Tom kept changing him from position to position—it must have been demoralizing for Timmy.

At one of our training camps Timmy and Tom had a bit of a run-in. Coach Landry told Timmy that he was stagnant, not progressing as he should. That upset the hell out of Timmy. Some of the guys on the Cowboys tried to make light of the situation and teased Timmy about it—all in the spirit of fun. That didn't do much good. Timmy was a real sensitive guy and Tom had really hurt his ego. Timmy walked out of training camp.

Not too pleased with that, Tom came in and blamed the players for what had happened with Timmy. "You teased him too much," Tom said. "That's why he walked out of camp."

But that wasn't the reason. Tom knows the reason. He was the reason. But he had to put the whole thing on us.

Benny Barnes's situation was similar to that of Doug

Donley. Benny played a whole year with an injured foot —it was injured so bad, most guys would not have played. Then Benny had surgery on his foot and it was all screwed up. But he worked his tail off in training camp, trying his best to get to play one more year with the Cowboys.

"Am I in the team's plans this year?" he asked Tom. "Just let me know. If not, let me go. Don't let me go to training camp and then cut me."

"Sure, we have plans for you," Tom told him. "Don't worry about it."

The training camp came to an end. And so did Benny's career with Dallas—they released him.

There were also a lot of guys with injuries who weren't told they had injuries or weren't told the exact nature of what was wrong with them. It was our bodies, our careers, but somebody else's advice on what to do with the injuries. I'm quite sure I had a lot of injuries that they didn't tell me about.

One time I was really hurting and was examined and told by the trainers that I had bruised ribs. "Man," I complained, "the ribs hurt too much to be only bruised."

"That's all it is, a bruise," I was told. "They'll get better, don't worry."

Around that time I was at the doctor's office getting a checkup, and the nurse let the cat out of the bag by accidentally telling me that I had cracked ribs. That pissed me off, how they tried to disguise what was wrong with me. All right, I lived with the cracked ribs and they healed in time, but I should have been told the truth.

A similar thing happened to Rafael Septien. He had a hernia. But they didn't want to tell him what he had because he was kicking so well and they thought it would affect him psychologically. Most of the season he was kicking away with that hernia needing treatment. After the season they finally told him what was wrong with him and said that he had to have surgery.

I had to have surgery once too. But I sure didn't want to have it done by Dr. Knight.

The surgeon for the Cowboys, Dr. Marvin Knight, was pretty old, and in my opinion his better years were long gone. A lot of the guys on the team called him "Dr. Knife." But even so, a lot of players went under that "Knight knife" because they were told by the Cowboys, "You have surgery by Dr. Knight or else we aren't going to pay for it."

Robert Shaw was a guy who should have had surgery but wound up not having it and that's a story in itself. A player who I thought could've been one of the best centers Dallas ever had, Robert messed up his knee in a game during his rookie season with the Cowboys.

They decided to hand him over to one of the Dallas doctors to strengthen Robert's knee. Instead of surgery they figured lifting weights would help get Robert's knee strength back.

After going through that conditioning program—some might say it was like putting a temporary Band-Aid on a bad injury—Robert Shaw was back in action.

In his second year in the league he was playing in a game and tore his knee up, and that finished him. In my opinion, if the problem with his knee had been fixed properly with surgery, that knee would not have been torn up and Robert Shaw would still be playing today and be an All-Pro center. But that was the way decisions were made about guys' bodies, the manner in which players were treated, sometimes without rhyme or reason.

Tony Hill is a good example of that kind of senseless treatment. One of my great friends on Dallas, Tony was in the habit of doing a lot of talking. But that didn't detract from his being a guy with a lot of talent. What I

remember best about Tony is all those times during our
rookie year, when we thought we should have been starting for the Cowboys, we would be sitting on the bench
just bored to death. We had to catch ourselves to make
sure we didn't fall asleep.

Every off-season, Tony would gain a lot of weight. But
he would always find a way to take it off as the season
got underway. Over the years, he had caught so many big
passes for the Cowboys. But the bloom was off the rose
with Tony and management, and he knew it. Tony sus-
pected he was soon to be released. He saw it coming.
One of the reasons was that he didn't get along very well
with our receiver coach, Paul Hacket.

When Tony came into mini-camp one year, they were
all very upset about his weight gain during the off-season
—even though they knew he never had a problem getting
those pounds off and getting into shape. "It's all bullshit,"
he told me. "It's an excuse they're using. They plan on
releasing me."

"How do you know that?" I asked him.

"Look at the press guide," he said. "It doesn't even
have my picture in it. That tells you something."

The word around was that the coaches felt he had lost
a little bit of his ability. But Tony should have been given
the benefit of the doubt, given an opportunity to show
what he could do. Instead they just let him go.

Almost from the start of the franchise's existence Tom
Landry, Tex Schramm, and Gil Brandt were in control of
the Dallas Cowboys. Pro football is a business in which
there's not much job security at the top, so it's very unusual for three people to have survived for as long as
they did.

Tom Landry would always say he was not management, but we all knew differently. In 1981, when people
pointed out that Tom was the only coach Dallas had ever

had, he showed he had a sense of humor. "That's one way to look at it," he said. "The other is I haven't had a promotion in twenty-one years."

But Tom was pretty high up there when it came to making the big decisions. All the players realized he had a lot to do with calling the shots about everything that went on in Dallas. If Tom wanted a guy signed, if he wanted a player to get X amount of dollars, if there were any snags or holdups in negotiations, the guy went to Tom, and Tom went to Tex, and it was a done deal. And there was no more said about it.

Not only did Tom have a great deal of influence in the day-to-day operations of the Dallas Cowboys—he also had his hand in every phase of what went on in that organization.

Gil Brandt, the director of player personnel, is a likable guy. You want to trust him. He'll smile at you, but you know he's got the knife ready, and when you turn he'll stick it in. Gil will do a lot of good things for you, but you know sooner or later he's going to fuck you.

I had my problems with Gil Brandt, but I still liked him, maybe because I always knew what to expect from him —a lot of guys don't. As long as you expect Gil to be sneaky you're okay.

Gil is not well liked around the league. When the scouting combines and get-togethers were organized by teams to look over prospects, and other scouts would come, Gil would be there acting like he was better than anyone else. Most of the scouts would get themselves a regular room in the hotel. That wasn't good enough for Gil. He'd come in and get a real big suite and throw lavish parties. That kind of behavior was designed to make some of the other scouts feel like little peons.

For a long time Gil did all the negotiating with the players for the Cowboys and it was his all-consuming interest. He sure was tough and a slippery man with a dollar. When I was having some financial problems and had to take some loans from the Cowboys, Gil negotiated it and I got the feeling it wasn't completely aboveboard. I'm still wondering whether that loan came out of my deferred money.

After my third year in the league, we were redoing my contract. And it seems to me that the part of the signing bonus that I hadn't taken up front just disappeared. And to this day I'm still ticked over the whole thing.

As the Cowboys became more and more involved in what the computer thought about athletes, it hurt them in the scouting area. After I joined Dallas there wasn't a top draft choice for many years who really contributed to the Cowboys. So Gil was taken away from negotiating contracts and was given the job of totally concentrating on personnel and acquiring talent, scouting college players throughout the country.

Tex Schramm, of course, was the top man there, the president and general manager of the Cowboys. Players on Dallas didn't have much of a chance to get too close to him. I guess because of all his power and his title they were afraid to do that. I spent time with him, though. I found him to be a pretty fair man and a pretty unfair man. He really knows how to deal with the media and is probably the best in the business at that. Tex is probably as much responsible as anyone in Dallas for marketing the Cowboys, for making them America's team, for giving them worldwide fame and visibility.

With the success the Cowboys have had as a franchise, with their attractiveness as a team, they've earned their reputation. But I think there's also been a little favoritism toward the team because of Tex Schramm. He's friends with Pete Rozelle and has a lot of power and lots of influence on what does and does not happen in the NFL.

Even when the Cowboys have been losing they've still
been on *Monday Night Football* and on national TV. And
a lot of that is due to his influence.

I have a lot of respect for Tex even though I know
there's a lot of animosity toward him from people around
football. Sometimes we had a love-hate relationship. But
you take the good with the bad. You can respect the guy
for what he's done in football.

V
SILVER AND BLUE

RELIGION HAS ALWAYS BEEN A PART OF THE COW-
boy mystique. But it was an image consciously created
by Tex Schramm. While there were some people, like
Clint Murchison and Tom Landry, who were very religious, the image of the Cowboys being "goody-good"
boys, the guys in the white hats, wasn't necessarily true.
The fact of the matter was that there were plenty of hell-
raisers on that team every year I played there. And there
are still some there today.

Now, Roger Staubach, who really *was* a guy in a white
hat, was in a class by himself. He was a true Christian.
People thought that because he was such a religious guy
he probably didn't have much personality. But he had a
lot of personality, and unlike most other guys, Roger
could have a good time without drinking, smoking, or
cursing. And one of the things I liked about him was that
he never tried to push his religion on anybody.

One of the best things about being in Dallas during my
first three years was coming into contact with Roger. I
told him that he was my hero, and I probably have more
respect for him than anyone I ever played with. I guess
it's a cliché to call him an officer and a gentleman, but
that's what he is. There were times when I thought if I
had been white I could have followed in Roger's foot-

steps in Dallas. I could have been the next Roger Staubach, and he and I could have wound up owning Texas.

Roger Staubach came to the Cowboys in 1969 as a twenty-seven-year-old rookie. Six years before that he'd been the Heisman Trophy winner out of the Naval Academy. The Cowboys took a chance on waiting for him to finish his Navy obligations and drafted him in the tenth round in 1965. Roger was sure worth waiting for.

A person with great leadership qualities, Roger had so much belief in his talents, in his ability to get the job done, that his confidence rubbed off on all the rest of us on the Cowboys. We felt if we could get the ball to Roger, we would win the game. And we did, time after time.

There are people who can handle success and those who can't. Roger was a guy who knew how to handle it, how to handle himself. Pressure was where he lived and where he was comfortable.

Our relationship was always very warm. Of course, we didn't hang out together—he was older than me, a family man with five kids—so I wasn't invited to the same things he was and vice versa. But we could always talk, share some funny moments, feel respect for each other.

Sometimes I would kid with Roger about the two of us running around town together and having a good time, but that was just to mess with him.

"You've got to go out with me, Rog," I would say. "Just think, man—if I had Roger Staubach with me there's just no telling how many women I'd be able to get."

"You've got enough as it is," Roger would fire back. The guy had a sense of humor.

Former Dallas quarterback Don Meredith got off the famous line: "I wouldn't want my kid to grow up like Roger Staubach. I'd want my kid to have more fun."

I disagree. If I had to pick someone for my son to grow

up to be like, I'd definitely pick Roger Staubach. The man
has class, the man has it all.

Out of all the quarterbacks I've ever seen I still rate
Roger Staubach as the greatest. He could always make
things happen with his scrambling ability and his leadership. Terry Bradshaw of the Steelers would come into the
huddle with Lynn Swann and John Stallworth. And John
would say, "Hey, man, I can beat this guy on this route."
Or Lynn would say, "I'm going to do this and that and go
this way." And Terry would call his own plays and they'd
do some creative things out there. On Dallas, only Landry
called the shots. Roger was great, but if he had been allowed to call plays like Terry Bradshaw during the course
of a game, he could have been even more phenomenal.

I saw Roger throw into coverages that Coach Landry
never thought could be thrown into. Roger's instincts and
his will to win, to excel, lifted the whole team. Like I said,
there have been and there are great quarterbacks in the
NFL. And maybe I'm a little prejudiced. But I still consider Roger Staubach the best I've ever seen.

Roger never asked for anything for himself, any special
treatment or favors. And he was the kind of man who
was always there ready to do anything he could to help
out other players. Although he played in the Dallas system, although he was the main man in that system, he
was never afraid to speak his mind. If there was a problem, some disagreement over something concerning the
team, Roger was one of the few guys there who wasn't
intimidated. He'd get himself on record.

Being with him on the Cowboys was something special.
The way we blended our talents—my running the ball
helping him; his passing the ball helping me—that's what
winning football is all about. We connected on a lot of
things and made a lot of things happen for the team.

One time when we really made something happen was

during the opening game of the 1978 season against the Baltimore Colts.

Roger threw me a pass out in the flat—I think the ball was tipped by a linebacker—and I had to do some fancy footwork and really look the ball in to snare it. Then I tucked the ball in, picked up some blocks from Tony Hill and Drew Pearson, and I was on my way to the end zone. I turned on the speed and lost all the pursuers. Coach Landry never said anything, but I'm sure he didn't like my giving and getting high fives before I ran the ball into the end zone. It was the only time I ever did anything like that in Dallas, but that was a special occasion. That pass reception and touchdown went for 91 yards—the second-longest pass reception in Cowboy history. Bob Hayes has the longest. So I guess we were entitled to high-five it a bit out there on the field.

Roger Staubach has said, "I don't think Dallas ever used Tony properly as a receiver. But I did in 1978." Roger and I clicked a lot that year. I caught about 45 passes as a receiver out of the backfield, and on quite a few of those passes I made some nice gains after the catch.

That 91-yard pass reception against Baltimore got me and the Cowboys off to a good start in 1978. The team won 12 of 16 games. I had six 100-yard-rushing games and piled up 1,325 yards—second in the conference, third in the league. In the playoffs I picked up another 484 yards rushing and five touchdowns. All of those stats were Dallas club records.

We made it to the Super Bowl for the second straight year. Two years a pro football player—and two years in the Super Bowl. It was an unbelievable feeling for me, knowing that I was once again in one of the biggest and best sporting events in America, a game that people watch all over the world.

Super Bowl XIII was played on January 21, 1979, in the Orange Bowl in Miami. The Dallas Cowboys against the Pittsburgh Steelers. I couldn't wait for all the pre-game hoopla to come to an end. I was ready to play. I was sky high.

But there was a lot of talking back and forth before we finally took the field. Thomas "Hollywood" Henderson kept teasing Steeler quarterback Terry Bradshaw. "If you spotted him the 'c' and the 't,' " Hollywood said, "Bradshaw would still have trouble spelling 'cat.' That's how dumb he is."

The guys on our Doomsday Defense made a lot of noise about what they were going to do to Bradshaw and the other Pittsburgh players. Both teams and both coaches—Tom Landry and Chuck Noll of Pittsburgh—entered that game with two Super Bowl victories. So the game was also for bragging rights as to which franchise and which coach would rack up a third ring. It was also the first Super Bowl rematch.

After all the hoopla the game was finally played and turned out to be probably the most exciting Super Bowl ever. The score was tied after the first quarter, and we trailed the Steelers by a touchdown at the half.

The way things happened for me early in that game, they've never happened quite the same way before or since. In our first possession I carried the ball three times, dancing and darting, for 38 yards.

Pittsburgh had a great defensive team. Those guys were called the Steel Curtain. "Mean Joe" Greene was one of the classic defensive players. But we were using Joe, running our plays off him, using him for me to get my yards.

Joe was one of the first nose tackles to set up about an inch from the center's head. And whenever Joe did that, he would cock his body one way or the other. Whichever way Joe went—that was the way our center would take him. And I'd then snap out of my stance, make quick reads, and I'd be slashing and shifting through the openings.

In that first quarter I carried the ball eight or nine times and piled up a lot of yards. Then for some reason Coach Landry stopped calling my number. I carried the ball very few times the rest of the game.

The game was like an aerial war out there. Staubach passed for 228 yards and three touchdowns. But Bradshaw, on that day, was even better, passing for 318 yards and four touchdowns.

With 6:29 left to play in Super Bowl XIII, Pittsburgh was ahead 35–17. And some of the Steelers were dancing and celebrating on the sidelines. It was an aggravating sight. We fought back, scoring twice in the final two and half minutes. Then with seventeen seconds left Rocky Bleier got his hands on our onside kick. That was it.

I wound up with 96 yards on 15 carries and 5 receptions for 44 more yards. We wound up losing 35–31. Terry Bradshaw was voted the Super Bowl Most Valuable Player. And Thomas Henderson snapped, "I rated his intelligence, not his ability." Then he continued: "Losing hurts . . . but what a show. They ain't forgetting this one for a while."

All of us on Dallas were disappointed at the outcome of Super Bowl XIII, but we looked forward to 1979 and getting to Pasadena and our third straight Super Bowl. With what we had—with what we were—it seemed we could accomplish anything.

Hell, we knew we were good. We had leadership, talent, depth, desire. Offensively, we had a great mix: top receivers, a super quarterback in Roger Staubach, and I represented the threat of speed coming out of the backfield. Defensively, we had all the weapons with Dooms-day II in operation.

We took pride in being Dallas Cowboys, playing Cow-boy football, being in the playoff games, the champion-ship games, the Super Bowls.

We demanded respect, earned respect. We had the re-spect and we had the fear. We could see teams out there just fearing us. In so many games, as we went into the last two minutes, the opposing teams had as much to do with their losing as we had to do with our winning. They just beat themselves.

Teams had so much fear of us, were so taken in by the mystique of the Cowboys, that they couldn't believe that they could stop us. They saw the star of Texas on our helmets, the silver-and-blue uniforms, the tradition of winning, dominating . . . and they were finished before they were even able to get started.

The franchise that was always the counterpoint to Dal-las was the Oakland Raiders. Whereas the Cowboys seemed squeaky clean wearing those tailored metallic-and-blue uniforms, the Raiders seemed mean and dirty in their black uniforms with the skull-and-crossbone insig-nia on their helmets.

Lots of people thought of the Raiders as a team that played outside of the rules, but I never saw them that way. I saw them as a physical team, a team with a lot of talent that played bad and rough out there on the field.

Lester Haynes was one Raider who was dirty, but in a different way. One of the greatest cornerbacks ever to play this game, Lester could cover his man. Stickum was a big part of his game plan. He'd put that stuff up and down his sleeves, his pants, his hands, get it mixed in with dirt and smear that stuff all over people. Dirty tricks were his specialty, and the way he used stickum was one of the reasons that they banned the stuff from the league. Lester not only used stickum; he wasn't afraid to use his hands, his knees, or any other part of him to gain an edge out there.

Jack Tatum and Lyle Alzado were big, physical guys. Tatum did his thing legally, but he seemed to like to hurt people. Alzado was mean and intense—legally or illegally—he loved to get his licks in.

The Cowboys were a reflection of Tex Schramm and Tom Landry. The Raiders were a reflection of their owner, Al Davis. His motto has always been: "Win, baby, win!" And Al always lets the guys on his team be themselves.

John Madden did a fine job coaching the Raiders. Although I didn't get to see him very much, I learned a lot about the way he coached from other players. There were all kinds of different individuals on those Raider teams, many unusual characters. Madden always seemed to be on top of his players' needs and made them all fit in and feel comfortable and be a part of the team. He knew all the coaching theory, but his great strength was letting his players play.

If you did something wrong in Dallas, if a player got himself into even a small scrape, there'd be all those cries: "Oh no, you're ruining the image of the Dallas Cowboys." But Al Davis has never been too worried about what his players do off the field, never been worried about team image. Al's concern, at the bottom line, is how his teams play football.

The Raiders have always had a lot of players on the team who were rejects from other organizations. Some people call those players misfits, but just because a guy has trouble fitting in with one system doesn't mean he can't play football. Many teams, especially the Dallas Cowboys, never wanted to be bothered with a player who had a problem in his past. The Raiders never thought that way. The crazies, the oddballs, the guys past their prime . . . the Raiders picked them up and put them on their team. The collection of characters, of guys with all these different backgrounds, helped contribute to the tough-guy, bad-guy image of the Raiders. That also made them an exciting team to play against and an entertaining team to watch.

In our division, all the teams we played against had different personalities and interesting characters, and that made for exciting rivalries. I can remember very distinctly how in my early years in the league Harvey Martin and Billy Joe DuPree and the others would go over the schedule with me: "Washington and New York will be real tough games, but you better buckle your chin strap a little tighter when you play Philadelphia. It's gonna be like a fight."

At that time Philadelphia was looked at as a team that was going to come out and try to beat you up and not worry so much about winning the football game. They were a real physical team. Bill Bergey was their middle linebacker. Out of Arkansas State, a perennial All-Pro, Bill was 6'3" and 245 pounds and presented a lot of problems for us.

Bill would try to intimidate me, and we had a lot of verbal altercations. In one game, he was working his mouth pretty good against me. When the game ended, he came over. "Tony," he said, "I didn't mean any of those things I was screaming at you."

"Is that so?"

"Yeah, those were just game taunts."

"Fine, man. As long as your bark is worse than your bite, there's no harm done," I told him.

But Bill had both a bark and a bite. He's one of the

defensive players that I still think about from time to time. The man was a hell of a football player.

The Washington Redskins, year in and year out, were the real challenge in our division. George Allen was the Redskin coach then, and there was a strong paranoia on the Dallas Cowboys about him. The week leading up to a game against Washington was "Redskin week."

"Keep an eye on all your stuff," our coaches would tell us. "Make sure you don't leave your playbooks lying around in your cars. Keep the doors to your rooms locked." That whole week, an air of suspicion and apprehension was everywhere.

Supposedly, before I got to the Cowboys, playbooks used to disappear during Redskin week. To prevent that kind of thing from happening again, Dallas scouts would prowl around the floors of the hotel, making sure that no one was moving around and spying on us. Sometimes they'd see people up there taking pictures and there would be confrontations. A lot of times a big deal was made out of nothing, but the atmosphere contributed to that. The problems were more about having your privacy invaded than anything else. But like I said, there was a paranoia about George Allen, a paranoia that was so powerful you could feel it.

The Redskins had lots of characters—Dave Butz, Billy Kilmer, and those types. They would make a lot of strong statements about Roger Staubach and the rest of the guys on our team, and it created a very intense rivalry. I thought It was a lot of fun. We really looked forward to playing them. We'd play one game in Dallas and one game in Washington. If we lost one game to them, then we knew there would be the revenge factor coming up in the second one. Man, we had some really hellified games with the Redskins.

The rivalry with the Redskins was so fierce that many

of the players on Dallas and Washington actually hated
each other. I wasn't involved in that part of the action.
When I had my Cowboy uniform on and they had their
Redskin outfits on, it was war. When I stepped out onto
the field, they were the enemy and I did everything in my
power to destroy them. But I also always kept what I was
doing in perspective.

Most of the time I was playing pretty much under control. I never allowed myself to get caught up in the frenzy
of all the shit, all the stuff going on when we played the
Redskins or some of the other more aggressive teams. I
realized what all the taunting was about. There would
always be people out there trying to distract you, trying
to make you get your mind on something else instead of
allowing you to play football.

There were guys who spit in the faces of other players.
I used to wonder how a player could spit at another. That
was disgusting. Even more, I wondered how some guys
could take that kind of stuff and not retaliate. There were
guys who would say really bad things about the wives,
the parents, the children of other players. It was pretty
rough stuff. I received my share of it too.

In one game against the Redskins I was running the
ball and was tackled hard by Darryl Grant. He out-
weighed me by more than eighty pounds and was on top
of me on the ground. It was something of a late hit, an
uncalled-for bit of extra punishment.

I was ticked off. Jumping up, I realized that I still had
the football in my hands and that Darryl was right there
beside me.

Pow! I slammed the ball right up inside his helmet.
Then Darryl started to come at me. He was a big, powerful guy, but I knew I could outrun him. I also knew that
wasn't quite the thing to do—not with the game on national television and all. So I made the decision to hold

my ground, to wait for reinforcements to arrive and the refs to blow the whistle. One good thing about the NFL— fights are broken up pretty quickly, if they even get a chance to start. Luckily for me, Darryl never got his licks in. With his strength and a full head of steam going, a guy like Darryl Grant could have killed me.

I had another close call in a game against the Redskins. Throughout that game a Washington coach kept scream- ing obscenities at me from the sidelines. Usually, as I said, I don't pay much heed to that kind of stuff. But this big, booming voice kept four-letter-wording it. I shot back my own special vocabulary to him.

As the game progressed, we both got more inventive in our use of language. Then, on a play that was a pretty big gainer for me, I got tackled into the sidelines. When that happens you sometimes don't realize where you are. I wasn't in no-man's-land. I might have been better off if I was. I was in front of the Washington bench.

Before I realized it, half the Redskin team was out there trying to put me away. Thankfully, that got broken up pretty quickly too.

When I run the football I stretch my eyes very wide, expanding my peripheral vision. My eyes light up like silver dollars. Against Washington, whenever I did that I would hear the taunt: "C'mon, bug eye! C'mon, bug eye!" Rich Milot, out of Penn State, and Neal Olkewicz would usually be the ringleaders in that taunting.

"C'mon, bug eye! Time for you to fumble for us!" They'd have themselves a time screaming those words whenever I had the ball. All their screaming did was give me a little extra motivation.

From the outside looking in, George Allen seemed to me to be a pretty intelligent coach and a strong mo- tivator. George got the most out of his players all the time. One of the big things with him was his respect for his older players—the guys who had been there with him through many seasons and contributed a lot to his success and the success of the Redskins.

When George Allen retired from coaching and a lot of the big-name players were no longer on the Redskins, all the glamour, glare, and intensity of our rivalry with Washington kind of disappeared. But then the rivalry kind of rekindled itself with the arrival of new players like John Riggins, Dexter Manley, and Joe Theismann. Those guys had talent, and they were also used to doing a lot of talking.

Dexter Manley made a big name for himself coming off the ball real well and being a great rusher. Joe Theismann was one of the cockiest quarterbacks I ever saw. He would do some things in the game and say some things after the game that I didn't particularly care for. But that was Joe. If you gave Joe the podium, he would keep it all night.

Maybe he had too much of the gift of gab, but he could get the job done for the Redskins on the football field. Tough to defend against, Joe was one of the first quarterbacks to work out of the floating pocket in Washington. He'd come out scrambling, throwing the ball. He was a fiery, intense kind of player, and I especially liked his competitive spirit, even if a lot of times he made us pay the price for it.

The Redskins had lots of guys who weren't afraid to say what was on their minds. We had some guys like that too—Harvey Martin, Tony Hill, myself. We would shoot back. It made for some good matchups, some great games, putting your money where your mouth was. That's what football is all about: the best playing the best. Lots of times both teams were at full force. All the guns were loaded and ready to be fired. It made it especially exciting on the field and it made it a good game for the fans.

I loved to play in RFK Stadium in Washington. The fans there, and they're great fans for the Redskins, were really behind their team. To come to Washington to that hostile environment and see a whole city crazy for the Redskins —it was an experience. Something I really enjoyed was coming into that stadium, scoring and quieting those fans down, and turning them around so they'd boo their own home team.

After the Redskins, coming up against the New York Giants was relatively peaceful despite their tough reputation. The Giants played hard, but they didn't do a lot of talking the way Washington did, except for a couple of players here and there.

Terry Jackson of the Giants and our Drew Pearson did a lot of talking to each other. They were always talking duels and deals. I just couldn't believe the kind of things they would be saying to each other. The Jackson-Pearson show would start as soon as they got out on the field. It was kind of like their own private version of the pre-game warm-up. And it never stopped until the game was over, sometimes not even then. They burned each other's ears, and the ears of those around them, pretty good.

In recent years the Giants have started playing a little better against the Cowboys. But in the first half of my career in Dallas, the Giants would somehow always find a way to lose to us. It was like we had their number.

A lot of times the Giants would be in control of the ball game, but we always felt we were going to come back and beat them. As long as there was time on the clock, we felt we'd beat them or they'd find a way to lose the game. And more times than not that's the way it happened.

Harry Carson created havoc for us before Lawrence

Taylor and Carl Banks even got there. I remember Coach
Landry saying, "If we can block Harry Carson, we can
run the ball." That was some "if." That guy Carson was
all over the field making tackles. Harry was a great
player, one of the best to ever play pro football. I sympa-
thized with him, seeing him play all-out, seeing his team
lose, seeing the look of disgust and disappointment on his
face so many times.

A couple of years ago the Giants ended up going to the
Super Bowl. That was a great year for them. But even
though they were dominating everybody else that year,
when they played us they had to struggle, even with Lawrence Taylor on the scene.

L.T. is the kind of player who shows just how much the
game has changed since I entered the league. Defensive
players like him are amazing. A dozen years ago in the
NFL you hardly ever saw 245-pound linebackers. Today
that's standard size.

But those guys are like freaks—bigger, faster, stronger
than ever before. It makes for some hellacious collisions.
I still enjoy getting out there and mixing it up with the big
boys, but the biggest boys . . . ? I'm not going to miss
getting my little body knocked around out there by those
humongous guys. I'll be watching, cheering like a fan and
not having any regrets that I won't be coming up against
guys like Lawrence Taylor.

Back in the era of a Jim Brown, Lawrence would have
been a lineman. He's so big, strong, powerful, and fast.
He's an incredibly dominating player.

When a team goes into a game against him, or players
like him—and there aren't many like him—the team has
to have schemes and plans aimed at just controlling Lawrence. He causes so much havoc out there that he
changes the blocking schemes used by most offenses. It
used to be that backs blocked linebackers. But a mere

back can't possibly block Lawrence. Tackles and other linemen are put on him. But they don't have very much success either. L.T. is such a great athlete he can contend with anything you throw at him.

In Dallas, the game plan for us was to run right at him rather than away from him. We felt that was a better way to go because Lawrence can come from behind with such great speed, pursuing the ball, stripping the ball away, making things happen. We also felt that Lawrence was conditioned to seeing teams run away from him, so our running right at him would at least make him do some adjusting.

On a personal level I've always liked Lawrence and rate him as one of the greatest defensive players in the league today. Yet with all that talent and desire, Lawrence had his problems. The drug thing and his admission that he was on that stuff surprised a lot of people. But it takes a hell of a man to admit to a problem like that and then try to clean house and put it behind him.

New York Giant fans are crazy. For quite a few years, this one guy always sat behind our bench whenever we played them. For a while he was always getting on Roger Staubach and Tom Landry. Then when Roger retired he switched to me. The guy was loud and vulgar, and he'd yell out, "You stink . . . you're a bum," and a lot of worse things. He'd be like a cheerleader for the other Giant fans, cheerleading ugly, trying to harass us all the time.

Although the fans in football are not as close to the action as they are in a sport like basketball, they're close enough. You can hear them pretty good. But I guess all that noise and profanity is part of the game. Players have to overlook that stuff and not get caught up in it.

The St. Louis Cardinals did not get many headlines playing in the division with Dallas. But they were a competitive team with quite a few top players. I always liked Terry Metcalf, a multipurpose kind of player. He was a tough and shifty running back, and he also filled the bill on punt returns. Terry was a guy who played all out.

Jim Hart was a great quarterback. When we went up against St. Louis, I used to love watching him play. Randy White, Ed Jones, Harvey Martin, and those guys would be barreling in on him, but Jim had that release, man. He'd just pick our secondary apart. He was a great pure passer. No mobility, but he could really throw the football. I don't think he ever got the full acclaim he deserved. He was much better than people thought he was.

During the 1979 off-season, I ran into Joe Greene and a few of the other Steeler defensive players in Pittsburgh. We got to rehashing the Super Bowl.

"How do you feel, Tony, about the way the game turned out?"

"Well, we didn't like losing, but we gave it our best shot."

"That's not the way we see it, Tony."

"How's that?"

"Well, we're glad Tom did what he did with you. To us you're the highest-paid decoy we've ever seen. If they'd kept running you in that game, we'd have had a tough time beating you guys."

That conversation kind of rubbed salt into a wound of mine. Throughout my career in Dallas, Tom Landry kept telling everyone that he regarded me as a "little back" and claimed he was conserving me. It was like he was doing me a favor, saving me to prolong my career.

We had a running debate over that issue. I could understand Tom's logic, but could not and would not ever accept it.

You use a guy only fifty percent of the time, sure, in

theory it's going to prolong his career. No doubt the way Tom used me I wound up taking fewer licks. But on the other side of the coin is the fact that for a running back any given play can be the last one of his career.

Your career can come to an end even in practice. William Andrews of Atlanta is a case in point. He was an outstanding back, a guy who had the ability to really explode through tackles. Then in practice he tore his knee up and that ended his career.

I'm the second leading rusher of all time in the NFL. Walter Payton is out there ahead of everybody else. But had Tom used me more throughout my career, I might have had a good shot at Walter.

When I was going into my twelfth season, someone told me that Walter Payton had carried the ball 1,100 more times than I had entering his twelfth year. I was astonished hearing that, for that's an awful lot of additional carries.

There I was in my twelfth season with a chance to go into second place behind a legend, Walter Payton. But if I had been given the chance to carry the ball as often during my early years in the league as some of the other backs, there's no telling what yardage I might have piled up.

All through the 1979 season, I was fighting the battle with Tom Landry about not running enough. I had a four-game streak with 20 or more carries a game coming into mid-season, but I carried the ball 20 times or more only once in our last seven games.

"I don't think it's unreasonable when I ask for twenty-five carries a game," I complained to Tom. "I've learned that it takes that many carries for me to get into the rhythm." He would always say that he had a plan, a reason, and that he was conserving me.

On the field that year we had another very successful

season, and we battled through the playoffs and came up against the Los Angeles Rams in the National Football Conference championship game. I rushed for 87 yards on 19 carries, but we lost a tough one to the Rams, 21–19.

That was a crossroads time for me and for the Dallas Cowboys. The game against the Rams was the last one for Roger Staubach. After eleven superb seasons the guy they called "Captain America" called it a career.

Through my first three seasons as a Cowboy, I had helped drive the Dallas offense by rushing for 3,439 yards. Now that Roger would no longer be a part of things, and with the void he created by retiring, I knew somebody had to step forward.

After Roger left we still had great athletes in Dallas. Danny White had bided his time and was now getting his chance. We had the Robert Newhouses, the Billy Joe DuPrees, the Drew Pearsons. It wasn't that we didn't have the offensive talent, but I prepared myself mentally to be the focal point, to be ready in crunch time when they needed somebody to win ball games. Thriving in pressure situations was always my thing. I looked forward to getting the ball when the game was on the line. I wanted to always be in situations like that, knowing that the pressure made me a better athlete.

It was during that time that I was made a co-captain. Being recognized as a leader meant something to me and made me feel that I had to prove I was deserving of that title. But I could have taken it or left it, for all it was worth in Dallas. On the Cowboys, all being a co-captain meant was having a title. Probably in other places, with other franchises, being co-captain would have meant much more. Coach Landry still did whatever he wanted to do. You'd go in and have your captains' meetings with the coaches and you'd say this and that about the team and the way things were going. But all that was just talk.

Nothing ever came of it. In other places, on other teams, what a co-captain said mattered. In Dallas, you were talking, just talking.

After the 1979 season ended I spent the off-season whipping and honing my body into the shape of a weapon—a weapon to win football games. During the 1980 season I tried to take a lot of the offensive pressure off Danny White's shoulders and put it on mine. We had another great year, winning 12 of 16 regular season games. I finished up with 1,195 yards rushing, becoming the first player in NFL history to rush for 1,000 or more yards in his first four seasons. I also scored 11 touchdowns and caught 34 passes.

In our final nine games (three of them in the playoffs) I rushed for 930 yards, averaging 5.3 yards per carry. On December 26, 1980, I racked up a team playoff game record of 160 yards rushing in a game against the Rams.

We came up against the Philadelphia Eagles in a divisional tiebreaker. In that game I only got to run the ball 11 times, gained only 41 yards, and we got beat 20–7. The whole thing was a downer. I know I didn't lose that game for us. But I didn't gain a lot of yards, and we lost. I hated losing after we had come so far that year.

Tom Landry said, "Tony was the best I've ever seen him in the games leading up to the playoffs and the playoffs themselves. Tony is now our catalyst. He's the one who makes us go on offense. If he doesn't, we're in trouble."

During the 1981 season I got my hands on the ball more than in any other year of my career and I made the most of my opportunities. I carried the ball 342 times for 1,646 yards rushing. Counting my years at Pittsburgh, that gave me a streak of eleven straight years of rushing for 1,000 yards or more. That 1981 season I had nine games in which I rushed for 100 yards or more. Then on December

13, 1981, at Texas Stadium in my fifth season with Dallas, I became the leading career rusher in Cowboy history. With a four-yard run around right end with 5:15 left in the fourth quarter, I broke the all-time rushing record of 6,217 set by Don Perkins in nine seasons. I was really proud of breaking that record, especially considering all the top backs who had played for Dallas—Don Perkins, Calvin Hill, Duane Thomas, Walt Garrison. What was also nice about that day was that we trimmed Philadelphia 21–10 and clinched the NFC East title.

Once again we made it through the playoffs and into the NFC championship game against San Francisco. We had that one pretty much under control. We had scored a touchdown and there wasn't much time left in the game, and they had to move the ball all the way down the field to score. We all thought they'd never do that against us. Our nickel defense was in there and we were expecting them to pass, but they ran the ball a lot and kept improving their field position. Then, with our defense pressuring Joe Montana and with good coverage on his receivers, Joe threw the ball away.

Dwight Clark came running out of nowhere and caught the ball in the corner of the end zone for a touchdown as time ran out in the game. San Francisco ended up beating us 28–27. That play, which everyone labeled "the Catch," turned their franchise around, sent them to the Super Bowl, and kept us at home again.

Joe Montana has a lot of field savvy and is the right quarterback for San Francisco's passing game, with all those reads going. Joe makes the read extremely well—one . . . two . . . three . . . and the ball is there. He protects his receivers and really delivers the ball, putting it right where it needs to be. One of the top quarterbacks to ever play this game, Joe Montana is a lot like Roger Staubach—never getting all the credit he deserves. People say that Joe doesn't have a real strong arm. They question his overall physical ability. But he's a survivor, a winner, and he lifts his team.

That last-minute loss against San Francisco was tough to live with and made for a long and unbearable off-season. If we had lost by a lopsided margin, it would have been easier to take. It was pretty devastating.

I was twenty-seven years old then and at the peak of my game. Through my first five seasons in the league I had gained 6,270 yards. Only Walter Payton and Jim Brown had gained more yards in five seasons. Going from nothing at Pitt to the national championship to the Heisman to the Rookie of the Year to the two Super Bowls to all the yards and moments of glory on the field—for me it was like a fast elevator ride up and up.

Probably the highest peak I ever reached was on January 3, 1983, in the last game of the regular season, against the Minnesota Vikings in the Metrodome on *Monday Night Football*.

Timmy Newsome was back for us to receive a kickoff. He got his hands on the ball and bobbled it, and we ended up on the one-yard line. Actually, it was the one-inch line. They don't measure in inches in football, but the tip of the ball was right there at the end zone.

Our fullback, Ron Springs, was in there in our one-back formation that we called the "Jay Hawk." I was on the sidelines since Ron was a bigger and stronger back than me. I felt Coach Landry was going to just try and punch us out of there to get some field position, some operating room. If we could get a first down I knew he'd come in with two backs.

I heard a play called, "31-fold," and I knew I was supposed to be in the game for that play. So I came charging in off the bench, running and screaming, "Ron, Ron, Ron! Get to the bench! Get out! Get out!"

Ron ran to the sidelines and out of the game, but that
left us with just ten men on the field. We broke the huddle
and people on the bench were telling Ron to get back into
the game. But seeing us come up to the line of scrimmage,
Ron wasn't about to run back onto the field and get penalized for not making it back on in time. So he just
stayed on the sidelines. Lucky, I guess, for me.

The Vikings were bunched tight in a short-yardage defense. I ran the play designed for Ron. Following a block,
I cut to my left to avoid some defenders and broke out
into the open field. I got down to midfield, and the only
players between me and the end zone were two Minnesota defenders and my teammate Drew Pearson. During
my years in Dallas, Drew helped me out a lot on my long
runs, knocking defenders out of the way. This time I
could see he was in some trouble. One of those pigeon-
toed types, Drew was running ahead of me but his legs
were becoming a bit wobbly. They were going every
which way. My thought was: Big Drew is going to run out
of gas.

I could see that Drew was probably going to be able to
get one Minnesota guy and put a block on him, but I
didn't know if I would be able to outrun the other Minnesota defender to the end zone. He had a good angle on
me. I figured he might be able to push me out of bounds.
That's when I made my move. I put the ball in both hands
and started pumping, trying to churn it out.

Turning on the afterburners, I went past Drew and the
two defenders. Drew made his block on one of them. The
other guy pushed me, but he was so beat from all the
running he had done that he didn't get a big enough shove
on me to move me out of bounds. I was able to maintain
my balance, stay in bounds, and run the ball in for a
touchdown.

I spiked the ball and started jumping up and down. I

knew I had run a long way. The first guy in to congratulate me was Drew Pearson and then other Cowboys came
running out.

It was only when I finally got back to the bench that I
realized what I had accomplished. I had run 99 yards—
the longest run from scrimmage in National Football
League history. It was a record, a record that can be tied
but never broken.

Accomplishing that 99-yard run was very meaningful
to me, especially the way it came about—just ten players
on the field, *Monday Night Football,* ABC-TV, a lot of the
nation getting a chance to see it all. It'll always be one of
my greatest moments in football.

I don't keep many trophies, but I wanted that one. After the game I tried to get the football. But the Vikings'
equipment man had tossed it back into the bag with all
the others. That got some headlines in the newspapers:
"Tony Dorsett Looking for the Football." And then for
weeks afterward I got letters from people saying they had
the ball. Most of the letters said the same thing: "Send me
X amount of dollars, and I'll send you the ball."

That was the up side for me. The down side for Dallas,
a down side that I always thought was pretty ludicrous,
was that because we didn't get to the Super Bowl, people
were saying we didn't have a successful year.

Once you've been to the Super Bowl you try to do everything humanly possible as a team to get back. You
work that much harder during the off-season to try to get
in position again to get into the Super Bowl. We tried and
came so close during those years, but it seemed, for one
reason or another, we just couldn't get over that final
hurdle. And each time we missed out, the more disappointing it got. It became incredibly discouraging for all
the players on the team. Looking back now, it was kind of
silly the way people felt. It was as if for us to be consid-

ered truly successful we had to get to the Super Bowl. Yet we were talented and successful and had all those outstanding seasons, all those wins. Teams to this day would love to be in that position and have all that success.

A lot of unfair criticism came about because of that. People were saying that we couldn't win the big one. Danny White, in particular, took a lot of criticism, unfair criticism. He had succeeded Roger Staubach, stepped into a situation where he was replacing a legend. Those were big shoes to fill.

All these years Dallas has been trying to fill the void created by the loss of Roger Staubach. Danny White has had a lot of pressure put on him with all the comparisons with Roger, and Danny has put a lot of pressure on himself. Even though he took Dallas to championship game after championship game, we didn't get back to the Super Bowl. Still, we won lots of big games with Danny as quarterback. I think he's a winner, but the media have always been on his case, saying he can't win the big ones.

One of the raps against Danny White has been that he doesn't have a real strong arm to air the ball out. But he's very smart. And he can read defenses better than any of the other quarterbacks Dallas has had since Roger. And that's a priceless talent for a quarterback. Later, when Gary Hogeboom joined the team, people began taking sides in the Danny White–Gary Hogeboom controversy. A lot of people stood up for Gary because he had a much stronger arm than Danny. Some of the players were also upset about Danny's role in the first players' strike. They thought he was too pro-management. A lot of people tried to pull me into commenting on who I thought should be the Dallas quarterback: Danny White or Gary Hogeboom. I stayed out of that controversy. It's funny, that's one of the few times I kept my mouth shut. But my thinking was that I wasn't coaching the team—it was Tom's decision.

Those may have been disappointing years for the Dallas Cowboys because we couldn't manage to get back to the Super Bowl, but they were also glory years. We were probably the winningest team at that time, America's team, the best football team around. There was all that TV exposure, the endorsements, the tradition, and the mystique was still magic—it was just mind-boggling that we could not find our way back to the Super Bowl.

My first six years in Dallas we could have—probably should have—been in six straight Super Bowls. After my first two years, though, we couldn't make it. We couldn't get past the Eagles in 1980, or the 49ers in 1981. The next year the Washington Redskins beat us 31–17 in the National Football Conference title game. You'd have thought that just through pure damn luck, we should have won one of those games. But it never happened.

The whole scenario then became a downward cycle. The better a team does in the NFL, the lower the team picks in the draft, so we always got low picks. Some say that was one of the reasons for the decline of the Dallas Cowboys.

Still, there was talent out there. We could have drafted better players. But we were drafting players who couldn't or wouldn't contribute. We could have traded for better players, picked up good talent that was waived, or signed free agents. Those things were hardly happening at all.

We were drafting players who came in and had short careers or never lived up to their potential. Rod Hill and Larry Bethea came in with a lot of fanfare, but they never worked out. Billy Cannon had some potential, and Robert Shaw, a guy who I thought would be a real good center, had a whole lot of potential. But both of them got hurt.

That's four guys right there who didn't do anything for the Cowboys.

In my rookie year I roomed for a time with quarterback Steve DeBerg. He could throw the ball, and I thought he had a lot of talent. Our number two draft choice that year was Glenn Carano. I have nothing against Glenn, but the Cowboys kept him because he was drafted so high and they let Steve go. Carano never developed into anything. Steve may have had a journeyman career in the NFL because of injuries, but he's still playing. I always thought that he should have stayed in Dallas and that he would have contributed to the team.

With no good new talent coming in, the players on the Cowboys started grumbling to each other; we were getting frustrated. We'd sit down and talk and wonder why we didn't get this player or that player. We'd see this big offensive lineman go to another team and become a star, and we knew we had had a chance to get him. We'd see that wide receiver go to another team and become All-Pro and wonder again why that guy hadn't wound up in Dallas.

I'm not saying this because we're both from Pitt, but I think that Dan Marino is the best pure passer in the NFL today. Dan has a great touch and a great release and he's one of the reasons the Dolphins lead the league every year with the fewest quarterback sacks. He's also very astute in his knowledge of the game. I saw Dan in his senior year when he came down with Pitt to play in Dallas in the Cotton Bowl. They played SMU. Standing tall in the pocket reading the defense, he was impressive. Even though he didn't have a great game that day, I could see even then that Dan was going to be great. I was telling my buddies, "This guy is going to be awesome in the NFL."

Dallas had a chance to draft Dan Marino but passed

him up. It was probably the best thing that ever happened
to him: he went to Miami, where Don Shula let him air the
football out. Tom Landry would never let Dan do the
things that he's been doing in Miami.

Don Shula is a coach I would have liked to play for.
Everything I've heard about him has been good. Don gets
the best out of his players, utilizing talent as well as anybody I've seen in the business. I have always admired the
way his teams perform.

Another factor that made the Cowboys lose talented
players was the team's mystique, its image—and trying
to make everyone fit that image. Not everyone can. We're
all individuals.

When Roger Staubach was there, he was a straight ar-
row, a clean-cut guy, Captain America. Players would
come in and get caught up in that and not really have
their own individualism. They respected Roger so much
that they didn't want to get out of line, and it sometimes
took away from their own natural personality. So when
the team would see a guy who was loud—and you need a
guy like that to keep you loose—you could hear, "Oh shit,
here comes that troublemaker," when all the guy was doing was trying to be himself and have a good time.

That image thing would always come into play. The
Cowboys wouldn't draft a player because their computer
spit him out. Maybe there was something in the guy's
past, or they thought he wasn't smart enough. They
wanted the intellectuals, the doctors, the lawyers, the en-
gineers—but a lot of guys who don't have book sense are
great athletes, with all the football sense they need. We'd
see those types of players go to other teams, even though
in terms of football they were as smart as anyone.

Dallas depended on getting a certain type of person,
with a certain type of disposition, a certain type of life-

style . . . all of that hurt the Cowboys' personnel decisions and helped grease their decline.

Sure, a team doesn't want criminals, but to reject guys because they had a problem in their past, or they had too much personality, or they might not be able to be molded into the image of a Dallas Cowboy—that was stupid. But that was happening time after time, season after season, and talent just slipped away.

Another thing that ultimately hurt the Cowboys is that Dallas played with emotion but not a whole lot of it. Of course, that was because we were a reflection of Tom Landry. Writers and fans would say, "The team plays like Tom Landry looks."

I'm not taking anything away from him as a coach who knows the game, but as a leader Tom was so damned cool, calm, and collected. I just couldn't see how a guy could get out there in a stadium with all that electricity flowing, all that excitement, all those great plays happening that were driving 60,000, 70,000 people crazy—and show so little emotion. Tom Landry had to feel *something,* but he sure didn't show it.

He was always strictly business, thinking about the next play, the next game. Being intense and unemotional is fine, but there's also a place in football for enthusiasm and for letting it all hang out.

Coach Landry's thinking was that jabbering and talking and threats were not needed. A lot of that stuff went on on the field with other teams. But he wanted us just to do our jobs and not get caught up in all of that kind of stuff. He never really said much on the subject, but the way he carried himself rubbed off on the Cowboys. The message was that his way was the way to act.

The Landry approach was that as an athlete you have to take it upon yourself to be ready—physically, mentally, emotionally—with whatever it takes to do a job out there. You were being paid to play; you were supposed to be ready. That was Tom's approach. His famous line was: "A team that has character doesn't need stimulation."

But I always thought he had more responsibility in all of that as a coach. When a team is not ready to play, when a team is not winning, when certain individuals are not up to par—then the coach has to do something to get things revved up. Coach Landry didn't see it that way.

We'd have guys going out there and making great plays on the field, scoring thrilling touchdowns or making long runs. But there weren't a whole lot of people busting their butts coming over to the players to congratulate them for what they had accomplished. It was their job to do that. That was the attitude.

You'd do great things out there on the field and come back over to the sidelines and there'd be a couple of comments and you'd sit down and wait for the next series. I went through a lot of that scene. It wasn't discouraging or disheartening to me. It was a way of life in Dallas. It was the way of the Tom Landry system.

When the Cowboys were winning, that approach worked and it was business as usual. But as the years went by and the team started to deteriorate, that approach became a problem. Because Tom was detached from it all, distant, and didn't show emotion, the players didn't show it either. But if we had played with a little more emotion, maybe just a little bit more emotion, we probably could have won more games than we lost in my later years with the team.

The Cowboys were the pioneers, the innovators, the cream of the league. As things got stagnant, as the talent supply slipped, performance went down and all of a sudden other teams in the NFL were catching up to us. And then they were passing us. There was a point in the decline when the Dallas Cowboys' mystique started to become a thing of the past.

A guy once gave me a line from Shakespeare that was about our faults being not in our stars but in ourselves. I've thought about that a lot in relation to many kinds of things.

In a way it applies to what happened to the Dallas Cowboys through the years. The fault, the decline of the team, from the top of the bill, was due more to the team itself than to its stars or its fate. It was its system that made the team great—going after the best athletes, using the computer, getting into all those innovations and routines, having the stability of the same group of people running things. But then, when other clubs started to catch up to Dallas, they were kind of stuck in their own success. They were resting on their laurels, continuing to do what they had been doing for so long, what had made them successful for so long. But the old ways weren't working anymore. Cowboy management didn't seem to see this, but what once had brought them success was now a good part of the reason for their decline.

VI
JOLTS

THE AMERICAN WAY IS THAT EVERYONE WANTS to be the best in whatever he or she does in life, and I'm no exception. I feel that I've been very fortunate to excel in the world of professional football. But ever since I was at Pitt, I have realized that celebrity has its minuses as well as its pluses.

Celebrity can be a hell of a hassle at times. People are drawn to you. People are always pulling at you, hustling you, saying, "We got this deal for you; we got that deal for you." And most of the time, they aren't good deals.

You meet all kinds of people and you wonder about them. What do they do for a living? Are they corrupt? Are they bad? Are they trying to hit on you? All of that comes with the territory when you're a celebrity.

When I go out to dinner I have to sit at a back table or eat late at night. Someone is always coming up. "I don't want to disturb you," he'll say, "but can I have your auto-graph?" People push their way over to you. They don't go away. They're standing there, talking, asking questions.

Then in a store, on the street, or in a movie theater, there's all the eyeballing:

"That's him."

"No."

"Too small. He doesn't look like his picture."

"Yes, he does."

"No."

"Yes."

"Let's find out."

Then the pieces of paper get shoved in your face.

"Sign this, Tony."

"Sign this!"

"One more now."

Sometimes I look at people like they're crazy. Who wants to sign shit all the time? Don't get me wrong, man. I think it's great that people think so much of me that they want my autograph. But people have to understand you don't want to be always signing your name and always having to answer all those questions.

Sometimes you want to be sitting down talking quietly with people, enjoying your privacy, having a good time, being yourself.

There are times when I don't want to be bothered by fans. Often I don't have anything to say or I don't want to talk. And that can create problems.

Sometimes I have felt like I could do without all the recognition. I just want to go out and excel and be appreciated for my talents, for what I do, for what I've done.

In our profession, being in the public eye is part of the territory, and giving something back to the public goes with the territory too. I try to always be friendly. But I also want a life of my own, a life where I'm not bothered and badgered all the time.

With all the crazies and freaks out there, I've become paranoid about people. Some are trying to stick a knife in your back. And there are always people around trying to use you.

I'm leery of strangers. I've gotten to the point, through some tough learning, where if I don't know who I'm dealing with I'll get gun shy and back away.

I have had cameras and mikes pushed in my face, and I've just had to deal with it. And I've gotten mud slung at me by the media, and I've had to deal with that too. I've learned the hard way how powerful the media are at making an image, at breaking an image.

When a player is out there in the public eye, the media magnify everything he says and run with it. They make a real big deal out of things that are not even worth discussing, just to sell newspapers.

I have been misquoted time and again. How I despise seeing words in print that I never even thought to say, let alone said.

Often I've said something one way, and when it appears in print it comes out another way, with words that give a different meaning to what I actually said.

The old expressions "Don't ever let the facts get in the way of a good story" and "Figures don't lie but liars figure" give a pretty accurate description of what I'm talking about.

I know reporters have to make a living, but I hate their taking advantage of someone's life, tearing it apart, exploiting things just to make a buck. Some of them think the way to move up in their profession is to pull somebody else down. That's why a lot of sports writing is at the expense of the athlete.

And some of those writers will come up to you the next day and smile and look at you like nothing's happened.

A media incident that still rankles me involved a writer named Skip Bayless. He came to Dallas from Los Angeles. Dennis Thurman, one of my buddies on the Cowboys, said, "Skip's a good guy, a good guy to talk to."

I spoke to Bayless for about ten minutes. We got along. Then the next thing that happened was a front-page headline in the *Dallas Morning News:* "Tony Dorsett— All-Pro Con Man?"

I read the article that Bayless wrote and was furious about it. He had put things in there that we never discussed. But that was a minor issue compared with a phrase he used—the racial slur "before we tar and feather him . . ." I've had the media misquote me, sure, but that line that Bayless wrote was a low racist remark. It gave me a strong dislike for him, to say the least.

Yet what Bayless did shows how an athlete, or any kind of celebrity, is at the not so tender mercy of the media. Bayless wrote what he wanted to write. I couldn't sue—I probably wouldn't have gotten anywhere. I couldn't go after him with a tire iron. That would have been satisfying, but stupid. I couldn't really do anything, but I made up my mind that I wouldn't ever talk to him again.

America loves athletes and athletics. The more successful you are as an athlete, the more people are curious about you. Maybe I was more successful, more visible than most players on Dallas. And maybe that's why less high-profile players could do whatever they wanted without having to read about it in the newspapers the next day.

As long as I didn't break the law it really shouldn't have been anybody's business what I did with whom or who I hung out with. That was my private life and not for all America to know about. If I wanted to be a hell-raiser, wanted to have a good time, it was nobody's business but mine, just as long as I wasn't hurting anyone. I didn't need to have that hot media spotlight on me all the time.

My success as a professional, like other players', did not come about through luck. People think it's easy, but it isn't. No one sees us in our winter workouts, or in our off-season programs, or sweating bullets in the hot sun running and lifting weights in training camp. All most people see is the finished product—the glamour and the glitter.

They don't realize what goes into creating a successful team or an outstanding athlete—the price that is paid.

And yet a guy's whole image, his professional reputation, all that he's worked so hard for, can be smeared and spoiled with one negative story in the media.

Back in the pre-season of 1983 my name was splashed across newspapers all over America in connection with a federal cocaine investigation. My name got the star treatment. But Ron Springs, Tony Hill, Harvey Martin, and Larry Bethea were all under investigation along with me.

The whole thing was a lot of bullshit. It pissed me off. None of it was true. I was not guilty of anything or charged with anything, but I was tried in the newspapers. Every day there was another story, and every day there was my name and my picture for all to see.

The whole drug charge was a case of making a mountain out of a molehill. A guy who supposedly worked for and lived with Harvey Martin was connected with the people the investigators were trying to associate us with. It was a case where people who were arrested threw names around to try to save their own skins. It was plea bargaining.

They knew that Ron Springs and Tony Hill and I were out a lot, moving here and there, enjoying our young lives. So they threw out our names because we were living life in the fast lane and were highly visible.

In the middle of July, when the investigation was still underway, our team was getting off a plane, and the players were all heading to their cars outside of the Dallas–Fort Worth International Airport.

Reporters started screaming out questions: "What's happening with the drug probe?" "Any news, guys?"

Harvey Martin turned to the reporters: "Don't talk to me," he said. "Don't ask me any questions. Go ask Tony Dorsett!"

I was shocked to hear that. I just could not figure out that shit that Harvey Martin said. It was like he was trying to incriminate me. To this day I can't figure out why he said what he said, the insinuations he was making. The way he acted and talked was all chickenshit.

If I were 6′5″ and 250 pounds like Harvey Martin, if I was even close to his size, I would have smashed his face in, whipped his damn ass.

I always knew that Harvey was somewhat envious of me, especially at the start of my career when I arrived in Dallas with all that fame and all those reports of the big money I was making. I always knew that he never cared much for me. I picked that up from the things people told me he said about me behind my back. But I never allowed any of that to affect the way I acted toward him. As long as he never did anything to me personally he could say whatever shit he wanted to behind my back.

Ultimately, the whole federal investigation was abandoned—it just faded away. No charges were ever brought against me. I was cleared of the whole thing.

But the stigma—the trial by the press—had left a stain. There was so much negative stuff in the newspapers that I have no doubt it cost me a great deal of money. A lot of advertising people were scared off because they were up in the air about the outcome of the drug investigation. I think I lost an advertising account with Brut cologne and a $100,000 endorsement contract with Lee jeans. To this day people are still skeptical, and even though I was cleared of all charges, sometimes I am asked if I was on drugs. As I said, it's trial by the press.

Drugs are in every part of our society—and football is just a small part of the society. But a lot of the headlines in recent years about drugs have involved football players. I don't know if drug enforcement authorities are cracking down so hard on the NFL just to show that they're doing something about the problem or what.

I can see how guys get into drugs through peer pressure or wanting excitement or trying to escape from problems. There are a lot of reasons for it. But what I don't understand is, with all the horror stories of athletes getting screwed up by drugs or dying from drug abuse, why anyone would continue to mess with drugs.

And now there's crack. I don't even know what it is, or what it looks like. But it's some powerful shit. They say you take it one time and you're hooked. My understanding is that's what happened to Len Bias with drugs. The dealers saw he was coming into some big money getting set for a long career with the Boston Celtics. They wanted to get him hooked to be his connection, to get rich off him.

The drug problem is pretty serious. There's also a lot of controversy and side issues involved with it, like drug testing. Personally I don't think it's the NFL owners' right to do drug testing. There are individual rights, too, that we all have as American citizens.

Without reasonable cause, I believe it's an invasion of privacy to just automatically check a guy out, like checking the oil in a car. But if a guy has had a problem and then if a coach sees some differences in his performance on the playing field, then there should be some monitoring. If there is no reasonable cause, it's not right just to pick on someone and say, "Okay, guy, today you pee in a bottle."

Drug testing is a real touchy thing. If a player says, "I don't want to do it. I won't submit. I have my rights," the owners say, "If you don't want to do it, you must be doing something wrong." The whole deal becomes a no-win situation.

But *something* has to be done about drugs. That stuff is

death. The Players' Association owes it to the league and to the fans and especially to the guys it represents to come up with some program to control drugs.

Steroids have also been around for years now and they need some looking into as well. I never had any interest in steroids. When I step out on the football field I want to be myself. But some guys feel they need to use steroids to get on top and stay on top, to enhance their performance, to become bigger, bulkier. The pity of it all is that I've seen guys become huge after using steroids but then later all the muscle turned into fat in the stomach.

There are a lot of unknowns and uncertainties as to what steroids can do to you. It's always been that way. Yet teams gave out steroids in the past, and coaches knew that players were using them. They didn't frown on it because the steroids were making guys bigger and stronger, helping put wins up there for the team.

Nowadays everybody is taking a second look at steroids because of all the possible dangers. I've always had bad feelings about steroids—it's unnatural stuff and it makes a guy into something he was never intended to be.

The drug accusation, all the notoriety and aggravation it brought, only goaded me to do my thing even more on the football field as the 1983 season got underway.

I had a big year running and even catching the ball. I led the NFC in rushing with 1,231 yards—77 of them coming in one exquisite run in Washington against the Redskins. I also caught 40 passes—the most in a season to that point in my career. Winding up the year in eighth place in all-time NFL rushing, I was named to the Pro Bowl for the third straight year.

Being in the Pro Bowl was always a great thing for me. I liked getting the chance to get to know and talk to people I'd been competing against. I liked getting different perspectives on the game from different players.

In one of the Pro Bowls I played in, Bud Grant of the Minnesota Vikings was the coach. I got to like him a lot. He was a good coach and a good person as well. An outdoorsman, a guy who liked to hunt and fish, Bud had an intelligent approach to training camp. He brought his players in about a week before the pre-season started— that was it. Bud told me he didn't believe in an overabundance of players or in overworking them.

Coaches like Bud Grant—who can discipline players, who can criticize them when they're doing bad, but can also pat them on the backside when they're doing good— coaches with that approach are the kind I like and the kind I think make for winning football teams.

In Dallas we were a winning football team that 1983 season, still posting a good record. But we couldn't get where we wanted to go.

We came up against the Los Angeles Rams in the National Football Conference wild-card game. They beat us 24–17 and eliminated us from the playoffs, ending our season right there.

Professionally, I was at the top of my game and feeling good about it. Things had gone well for me on the field, and I looked forward to 1984. But on the personal front, it would turn out to be a pretty bad year.

For one thing, my wife, Julie, filed for divorce that summer. It was no surprise; things between us hadn't been good for some time. We had been married for a little more than three years. At first it was great, but then things had started to come apart. I got married, I see now, for all the wrong reasons.

Living life in the fast lane had brought me into contact with so many women, yet with all of them around, none of them really meant much to me. The scene got tiresome

—waking up in the morning and finding myself lying next
to someone I knew I didn't want to share my life with. All
those women, all those times. It got so I couldn't wait
until they left in the morning.

Then I met Julie Simon—a girl from California. We hit it
off right from the start. She was dynamic, she was beautiful, she seemed right for me. I loved her, or at least I
thought I loved her. On my twenty-seventh birthday,
April 7, 1981, we got married.

Julie had a three-year-old daughter then, Shukura. The
weekend Julie and I were going to go to Hawaii on our
honeymoon, Shukura was going to visit her natural father. But then we got the news that he was killed in a car
wreck. It was an awful thing. The upshot of it all was that
I became like Shukura's father. She started to call me
"Daddy" and I loved it.

I would come home from a hard day's work and
Shukura would hear the door open and I'd hear her little
feet come pitter-pattering down the hall. She'd jump on
me. "Daddy! Daddy!" And there'd be those sweet kisses.
I loved that little girl with all my heart.

That relationship caused some conflict with my son's
mother. She thought I loved Shukura more than I loved
my son.

"Look," I finally said, "Shukura is with me constantly.
She loves me and I love her. I love the heck out of her and
I'm not going to deny it. You can make what you will out
of it." That ended the discussion as far as I was concerned.

As I said, my marriage to Julie was wonderful at the
start. But as time went on I couldn't believe she was the
same person I had married. There is something about
marriage and that piece of paper, that "I do," that makes
people change. I've heard that line over the years, but
you have to experience it to understand it. I didn't like

the idea of being asked a lot of questions, where I was, what I did . . . I didn't like being quizzed. Julie did a lot of listening to her friends: it was like a train was blowing in her eardrums. "You oughta do this. You oughta do that."

It was getting to the point where I was thinking if she wasn't going to file for divorce, I was going to do it. And I knew there were very few nice divorces. In August of 1984 I came back from training camp to our nice, big, beautiful home, and she told me she didn't want me living there anymore. She said she was afraid. I knew I had to move out and I hated it. It was like we both woke up one day and finally decided that we didn't want to be married. The divorce came through in 1985—a $250,000 cash settlement plus my Mercedes.

Marriage was probably the worst mistake I ever made in my life. It wasn't necessarily Julie, but it was definitely the wrong thing for me to do at the time. I didn't get married because I was in love. I got married because I was lonely. And I paid for it. I paid for the loneliness, goddamnit. The sad thing is that I knew the marriage wasn't going to work when I entered into it. I knew it wasn't going to last. I've always had a tendency to do some things I really don't want to do. A lot of times it's hard for me to say no. That was part of it all too.

One of the things that all professional athletes dread is getting a phone call from home out of the blue during practice or a game. In October of 1984, I was at a practice and I got that kind of call. The message was from my brother Ernie, and it was simply: "Call home."

I didn't really think much about it. It's funny the way things happen. My dad and I were just starting to get close after all those years. I'd always gotten along well with him but had been much closer to my mother. The

day before I got that call I had phoned home, wanting to
talk to my mother, but since she wasn't there I'd spoken
to my dad for about half an hour. I was going through my
divorce then, and he thought I was living in some small
room somewhere. He hadn't known that the townhouse I
lived in in North Dallas had three bedrooms. Somehow
that came up in our phone conversation.

"You know what, Tony," he said. "I'm going to take
some time off and come on down and be with you. I'm
coming to Dallas."

"That will be great, Dad," I told him. "We can go out
and spend time together and talk."

When I got the phone call on the practice field, I
thought that was what it was about—my dad's plans to
come to Dallas. So I figured I could wait until the practice
was over and then I'd call home.

Gene Stallings, now the Phoenix Cardinals head coach,
who was then one of our assistant coaches, heard about
the message. "If I were you, Tony," he said, "I'd call home
right now. You can never tell about those calls. Maybe it's
important."

I went to the trainers' room and made the call and
that's when I got the news. "Tony, your dad has suffered
a massive stroke," my mother told me. "It was pretty
bad."

I couldn't believe it. I had just spoken to him the day
before, and he was in very high spirits and said his health
was fine. I couldn't control myself. I put my head in a
towel and cried and cried.

I left the practice field, rushed to the airport, got on a
plane, and flew to Pittsburgh. By the time I got to the
hospital in Aliquippa, my dad had lapsed into a coma. I
saw him there, down on his back on the bed. That was
tough. My dad was such a strong man. To see him like

that, so helpless, with all those tubes running through him
—it broke me up.

My mom was with me, anxious to talk, to tell me all
about it. "He was at the doctor's only a few days ago,"
she said, as if she couldn't quite believe what had happened, "and the doctor told him his blood pressure was
real high. He had to take his medicine, but you know how
Dad is, he wouldn't take his medicine unless you were on
top of him.

"On Sunday morning," she continued, "I was downstairs, and he was upstairs about to take a shower. He
had to eat before he took his medicine, so I told him I
would fix him some breakfast as soon as he came out of
the shower.

"Ernest was in the other room. He heard Dad call out,
'Teeterbug, Teeterbug, help me!' [Teeterbug is my brother
Ernie's nickname.] Ernie ran into the room and found him
sitting on the floor in his underwear. He came running
downstairs to get me, saying, 'Mom, something's happened to Dad.'

"I ran upstairs, Tony, and it was an awful sight. Big
sweat was coming out of his forehead. 'Wes, what's
wrong?' I asked. It was getting so he couldn't talk. He
only said, 'My . . . head.' I thought: Oh Lord, what are
we going to do? How are we going to get him off the floor?
He's so big.

"So I said, 'Teeterbug, you go get his house coat and
house shoes.' We took him under each arm and dragged
him down the stairs and into the car. We put him in the
front with Teeterbug, and I stayed in the back, holding
him up.

"Tony, Tony," she said, "God works in strange ways. If
Teeterbug hadn't been there with us, Dad would have
died in the house. Only I didn't know how bad it was. I
didn't know he had such a big stroke. If I had known that,

I would have talked to him on the way to the hospital. I was quiet because I knew his head was hurting him so bad. And the next thing we knew, he was in a coma."

I was trying hard to comfort my mother, but it was rough. Scenes were passing before my eyes, like the time I went to the steel mill to get the keys and he was so covered with dirt I didn't recognize him. I thought of how proud of me he was when I won the Heisman Trophy. I thought of all the laughs and jokes we had together. And I thought of the way he called me "Hawk"—it was his name for me before anyone else's.

I spent just a day in Aliquippa and then I returned to Dallas and was out there on the football field having to do my job and get myself up and at the same time deal with the situation. It wasn't easy, but I guess it was easier on me than on the other family members, since I could play and keep busy.

We played the Giants and I ran for my father. I gained 78 yards. Remembering how he felt about me and how proud he was of me enabled me to keep going. I knew he would've wanted me to keep going. All through that game he was on my mind. Not many problems have ever followed me onto the football field, but I thought about him during the huddles, during the time-outs. I thought about him all the time.

I went back to Aliquippa a couple of times just to be with my family. You know how it is, how all the people in a family huddle together in times of crisis. When I was there, though, with all the memories, I couldn't sleep. I'd be awake all night tossing and turning. It wasn't so much that I wished I could have said this and that to him, but I kept remembering how he used to talk to me about what it was like working in the mill and how he didn't want me to end up there, how modest he was when people asked him about me, how much he liked kids, how he used to treat strange kids like they were part of his family. It seemed there wasn't a kid in the neighborhood who didn't know him well enough to call him "Uncle Wes."

I was about to leave Aliquippa for a game, and I said to my mother, "I'm going to play this game for Dad, and then I'm coming back. He'll be all right as long as he's on the machine, won't he, Mom? God can work miracles."

"Yes, He can, Tony," she answered, "but when your time is up, He's going to take you anyway."

"He'll be all right till I play this game," I said.

"Tony, your dad's dead already."

I looked at her like I didn't want to believe her. We had been through this before. She told me that Dad had always said that if anything were to happen to him and it became a choice of his becoming a vegetable or going out with dignity, his wish was: "Don't keep me alive, just let me go."

I knew she believed it was just the machines that were keeping him alive, but I wanted to hold on. "Let's not rush, Ma," I would say. "Let's give him time. He's a strong man, he's only sixty years old. How can anyone be sure he won't make it?"

Before I left, though, I told her, "When the time comes, Ma, it'll be your decision, not mine, not any of the other kids', just yours. The man has been with you much longer than he's been with us."

It never came to that—pulling the plug. By the time I played that game, my dad was dead. Still, if it had come to that, to pulling the plug, my father's wishes would have been the deciding factor. A man as strong as he was, a man with as much pride as he had . . . it wouldn't have been right to let him waste away. It would have killed all of us just looking at him and knowing he was being kept alive just for the sake of being kept alive.

The game we played right after my father died was

against St. Louis. It was November 4, 1984. We beat the
Cardinals 14–10 in a crucial game. I gained 84 yards, a lot
of them twisting, darting yards, making something out of
nothing. And right after the game I returned to Aliquippa
for the funeral.

All the way home I thought of my father and what his
life had been like. I'm not a very emotional person except
when it comes to my family. And the death of my father
took a lot out of me, for a long time. Of course, death hits
everyone. But when it happens to you, you become selfish and ask, "Why me? Why me?"

There were over three hundred people at the funeral. I
knew my dad was well liked, but I never expected to see
that many people. There were as many downstairs as in
the chapel upstairs, and there were still more people outside. Many of them were from the old days: Coach Butch
Ross, some of my high school buddies, people from Pitt. I
didn't think anyone from the Cowboys would come, but I
was wrong. Tex Schramm was there representing the
team. It was so unexpected. Tex's coming to my father's
funeral showed me the type of man he is way down deep
inside. He didn't have to make that long flight to Pittsburgh from Dallas, make that drive up to Aliquippa to be
there. It really touched me, and after that I looked at him
differently.

The following month I had a close call that made me
think of my own mortality. It was in Veterans Stadium in
Philadelphia. I was running full out to my right following
my offensive linemen. Ray Ellis, the Philadelphia safety,
came charging at me.

I didn't see him. Boom! He knocked the mess out of me.
My helmet flew up—it could have flown off if I hadn't had
my chin snap fastened tight. But the power of that shot
knocked me out instantly. I went down on the ground in a

heap. I didn't feel the hurt as much as other hits, I guess, because when you're knocked out you don't feel anything.

A bunch of guys came running out onto the field. I was down on the ground, flat out, trembling, quivering, and my eyes had rolled up into my head. "He's seriously hurt," I heard one guy say. "Tony's gonna die," I heard another one say. "He's gonna be crippled," I heard someone else say.

I found out later that Ray Ellis had come over and sat down by me and said a prayer. Somehow I got back to the sidelines with a little assistance from my teammates.

Back on the bench I looked out on the field and was confused. The Eagles had the ball. "What happened?" I asked. "Don't we have the ball?"

"You fumbled, Tony," I was told. "But that was the least of it all. We thought you were finished; you took a wicked lick."

Probably no one thought I would go back in that game, but I did after I was examined at halftime and responded. I was still a bit dazed, but I was okay.

Back in the game, I was hesitant at first, not knowing what would happen if I got hit. But I got into it all right. If you're as tough as you think you are, you can go out there and play after those types of hits. I've been pretty fortunate to have been able to go out there and kind of forget about things and get on with my job.

The funny thing was that I kept running this one play that we had planned out, but I was running it wrong. However, it turned out all right. I was taking a counter-step when I wasn't supposed to. Doing that helped me rush for over 100 yards in the second half. And we ended up putting that play into our offense.

After the game I was interviewed about the hit on CBS-TV. They wanted to review it; I wanted to forget it. They ran the tape of the play. Man, I shuddered seeing it. It was devastating, like being hit by a car.

As bad as 1984 was for me personally, professionally it was probably my best. Right from the early days of training camp I knew that as a team we had gone down a notch. The kindest thing that could be said about our offensive line was that it was poor.

I had to search out cracks in the defense, slip and slide, dance and dart my way around on the field to get my yards. Man, those yards that season were tough coming. Bouncing off guys, fighting my way through cracks, doing my spin moves, innovating—that's the way I had to operate game after game.

The yards kept coming in little gainers—three yards here, four yards there. I also caught 51 passes that year— a Cowboy record for receptions. And when I caught the ball I nibbled off, tacked up some more yardage.

My longest run of the season was just 31 yards, so when I looked up after all the dancing and diving and saw 1,189 yards rushing for the season, I knew all those quick-hitters and stutter-step moves had added up.

I had passed Jim Taylor and Earl Campbell to climb into sixth place on the NFL's all-time rushing list. That gave me a lot of personal satisfaction and was something I knew my father would have been pleased to see. But as a team we slid back some more, missing the playoffs for the first time since I joined the Cowboys. In fact, it was the first time Dallas wasn't in post-season play since 1974.

We players were tough on ourselves when the team started to slip. But with the media, it was another story. Back then the Cowboys had so much clout that the media were afraid of the organization's power. There was an awful lot of control over what the media would say or write about certain individuals or the franchise itself. The

Dallas Cowboys were like gods in Texas, put up on a pedestal. To take a shot at Tom Landry or Tex Schramm or the franchise itself was unheard of back then.

The media were also being managed, living high on the hog. They were flying on the charters, being put up in hospitality rooms and suites. Some members of the press were "getting the scoop" before others. I'm quite sure those "goodies" were things that the media didn't want taken away from them.

Ultimately, though, the press had to deal with the fact that the Dallas Cowboys were not what they once had been. That's when all that stuff about the image came out.

People today say that the image of the Cowboys has changed, but that's not true. The Cowboys are doing the same things they did before I got to Dallas, while I was there, and now that I'm gone. It was just that when the team was winning, the media would not write about those things.

Just as the great success of the franchise over the years affected the way the media looked at it and covered it, that success also had an influence on the guys who played for the Cowboys. It also affected those who played against us.

Opposing players not only disliked the franchise, our coaches and players, some even complained about our fans. They just hated everything and everyone associated with the Dallas Cowboys. Guys on opposing teams didn't want to be around Cowboy players even in the off-season.

I found all of that rather amusing. Football is football. When I came home, I left football on the playing field. In the off-season, I was off. But there were guys who let football consume them all year round and carried the whole thing to ridiculous extremes.

Some of the guys on the Dallas Cowboys were like that

too. When we were piling up all those big winning records, the atmosphere around the team was up. Then when the down cycle began and the winning became less easy, the atmosphere started to change. Guys became testy and surly.

On Dallas, and probably on every other team, there were guys who took the game home with them. If they had a bad day or if the team lost, they would become abusive and take it out on their wives and families. I hated to lose, probably more than anyone, but I always kept the game in perspective. It was a game and a business. You tried your best to win and excel. But that was not going to happen all the time. And you had to keep your bearings on all of that or the game would consume you.

One time, we had lost a game, I think it was against Washington, and we were flying back to Dallas. I was sitting in the back of the plane with a bunch of guys, and we were playing cards. A few of the guys were laughing about the way the card game was going.

About midway through the flight I got up to go to the rest room. Don Smerek and Jeff Rohrer and a couple of other guys were standing near the rest-room door.

"Excuse me," I said. But no one moved out of the way.

"Excuse me," I said again. "Is the bathroom free? Can I get in?"

"No," Rohrer answered, "you can't."

"What do you mean I can't? I've got to go to the bathroom. Move out of the way, guys." I thought they were kidding around.

But Smerek and the rest were serious. "You were up there laughing at Coach Landry," one of them said.

"Wait a minute," I said. "I wasn't laughing at Coach Landry. You don't know what the hell we were laughing about. That doesn't make any sense. What the hell would I be doing that for?"

"You're the ringleader," Smerek said. "And you've got those guys under your thumb."

I was starting to get angry. "Look," I said. "You don't know what the hell you're talking about. I'm going into the rest room to make my water deposit and then I'm coming back out."

When I came back out they were still there in their little mob scene. "Dammit," I said to them, "there's nobody on this team who wants to win football games any more than Tony Dorsett. But there's one thing you have to understand. This is only a game. I don't eat, live, and sleep football. I don't take this shit home with me—win or lose. If we lose, I'm realistic. I understand you're going to win some and you're going to lose some."

But those guys kept on making a big deal about the loss and the laughing and their belief that I wasn't good for morale and a lot of other shit like that. They started to get pretty hostile. One of the flight attendants tried to get in the middle of it, but she was blocked out. Smerek challenged me and tried to take a step at me, like he was going to scare me.

I didn't bat an eye. "Look, man," I said, "you may be much bigger than me, but you don't scare me. I don't know who you think I am, but you don't put any fear in my heart."

Smerek was all puffed up and started to spit out profanities.

"I wasn't brought up to take any shit," I told him. "But I'm not going to fight you. If anything, I'm going to kill you first."

Don Smerek had been blown away before. Once he tried to take somebody's parking space. The guy showed him a gun and it ended up with Don being shot. He almost died.

"If I shoot you," I said, "you're not going to be standing here and telling anybody about it. I'll take care of you for sure."

Nothing much came out of that encounter. But that incident showed how the game could consume guys, make them hostile and mean and miserable. I'm not going to call out any other names, but the way some of them acted was just ridiculous. Preparing for games, I've become a little irritable, not wanting to talk, things like that—just trying to get myself in the right frame of mind. But to have the game warp your personality, make you hostile and angry—that was bullshit.

In the mid-1980s, I felt like I was a lightning rod because as each year went by, I would get hit with a jolt. It gave me lots of practice in learning how to cope, how to survive. There was that bullshit drug charge and the incident with Harvey Martin in 1983, then there was the divorce suit beginning in 1984, and just a few months later my father's death. All of those things took their toll on me, especially losing my dad. But in the summer of 1985, it was like the jolts were coming one after another. And it was all I could do just to get through.

That summer of 1985, things were caving in all around me. I compare that time to running through life with a football in my arms and at every turn, from every angle, getting a bump, a shot, a hit.

I was saying to myself: What else can happen? I was reeling from it all. It was like being out there in the open field getting hit on all sides by big burly linebackers. Maybe it would have been easier on me if linebackers were my only problem. But what I was reeling from was a mess of financial shit.

One part of the mess came through my agent Witt

Stewart's dealings with Ken Tureaud, a Tulsa business-man. Tureaud was trying to act as a go-between to get me to join the Los Angeles Express in the USFL. Somehow Tureaud offered Stewart options on stock in an oil-explo-ration deal. When Stewart told me that he was going to get into those investments for me, I listened. Then I asked, "Are you sure about this?"

"Yeah, yeah," he said. "Don't worry about a thing. We got it all under control."

"I'm not worrying," I told him, "but if I lose my money, I'm going to kill you."

I got my money together: $238,000 from a deferred-pay settlement, $175,000 from a loan from the First City Bank of Richardson, Texas, and $107,000 in cash that I had on hand.

The deal didn't work. Stewart later admitted: "I went crazy. Tureaud told me we were going to make three to four million dollars in ninety days. I was a charging bull. I didn't see the sword. I was blinded."

Gil Brandt might have been right when he said that all my troubles came "because of the incompetent people Tony surrounded himself with. They might have done fine things for other people, but they were not doing things in the best interests of Tony Dorsett."

I don't know whether Witt Stewart got snowballed or what, but the whole deal upset the hell out of me. It was a mess, a whole pile of trouble. Of course, I didn't kill Witt Stewart, but I felt like it. I lost an awful lot of money, my hard cash money, and then the money I borrowed. We're talking big figures here. I was told that I'd get the money back, and I'm still waiting.

In the middle of all that, I was hit with another jolt. The IRS claimed I owed $414,247.91 in back taxes because a tax shelter that I had invested in was disallowed. The shelter had been recommended to me. It was a popular thing in the late 1970s when I got into it.

To satisfy their claim, the IRS garnisheed my Cowboy paychecks and placed liens on my houses—one was worth $800,000 and the other $280,000.

Losing all that money in the oil deal, getting hit with a lawsuit by the First City Bank of Richardson for the loan they made me, having the IRS on my back—all of that made 1985 a hell of a year for me. But I wasn't broke. I was still helping my friends out, loaning five or ten grand here and there. I even co-signed a lease for a computer store for a buddy of mine. But the guy couldn't make the deal work. When all the dust settled, I was out another $48,000 and, would you believe, fifteen autographed footballs.

There's a lesson in what I went through for all professional athletes. I would tell them not to try to get the pie in the sky. Don't try to hit the big one. Surround yourself with a good team, people whom you can trust. Realize that the wealthiest people in the world lose money, but realize also that you have to be conservative and know where every dollar goes.

I've had my moments with agents. When I was playing for Pitt I was represented for a short time by Nelson Goldberg. Then I was with Don Cronson and then Mike Trope.

I don't have anything too positive to say about Don Cronson. There are a lot of mysteries surrounding that man. He's involved with Ed "Too Tall" Jones, and sometimes I think they're in cahoots. I never had any real trust in Don Cronson. But he gave me a song and dance that it would make things simpler for him if I gave him power of attorney over some monies. And I gave it to him.

The next thing I knew I got a call: "I put this money in this . . ."

And I said, "What did you do?"

"It's okay," he said.

"Just because you say it's okay," I said, "doesn't mean it's okay."

And then he wanted his fees for doing things I never told him to do.

"Wait a minute, man," I said. "You're moving too fast." The guy was dealing but he wasn't cutting the cards.

I guess like some other athletes I've been unfortunate and made the mistake of letting some people I've trusted fuck me around. But life is a growing experience. If you don't learn from your problems, you die. I like to think I've learned something from all I've gone through.

Money, as the old saying goes, is the root of all evil. And there are people out there on the make just lusting to take advantage wherever they can. A player is represented by someone. The player gets busy and caught up in so many different things that he doesn't have time to check on what is happening with his finances. And if there are con artists or unscrupulous types around, that's how the trouble starts. When you make a lot of money, you open yourself up to the possibility of being ripped off or swindled.

People always ask why the teams don't help their players out with financial advice and money management. It's a good question with an easy answer. Most teams don't want to do that. It's kind of a conflict of interest if they pay you and then tell you what to do with your money. But the bottom line on that issue is that teams want you totally dependent on them. In Dallas, for instance, very little was done to set players up for their lives after football. Players wanted to go to school. Dallas management said, "You can graduate later. We want you here now. Forget about school until after your career is over."

The Players' Association has been trying to help guys

out and protect them from the bad agents out there by
checking them out and licensing them. That's good. But I
also feel that the Players' Association owes it to the guys
to have a program for investment so that players are not
totally dependent on the franchise.

As for me, today I'm with good people—I trust them.
They're first-class people. But if somebody ever again put
me into the financial shit I was in, that somebody would
have to pay dearly in one way or another. I tell people:
Don't fuck with me. If you need something from me, ask
me. Don't take!

My financial problems with the IRS that summer were
just one of the storms I was in. When it rains it pours, and
it poured a lot that summer. I was also holding out from
coming into training camp. One thing had nothing to do
with the other, although there were people who were trying to make it seem that way.

The background on the holdout began after the 1984
season ended, when I learned that Randy White and a
bunch of other white guys were being set up for many
years to come by the Cowboys. They were getting their
life-after-football taken care of by new contracts with
package deals that contained annuities. I felt that was
treatment I was also entitled to, and I was determined to
get it.

When you're an important part of a team's success and
certain individuals are getting security and you're not,
you want to know why. You want a piece of that action.
My mind was made up to renegotiate my contract before
the start of the 1985 season.

I did some talking with Gil Brandt, and he was hem-
ming and hawing all over the place. I knew what he was
telling me was just meant to appease my agent and me.

"Don't worry about anything, Tony," Gil said. "We're

going to take care of it. We'll renegotiate after the season is over."

"I want to do it before," I told him. "I'm adamant about that."

"We'll have more time later, Tony. Let's leave it for then."

One of the things that bothered me most about that whole situation was that it seemed the white guys on the team were getting the royal treatment, the annuities, the bigger money, and being taken care of for their life-after-football, and the black guys were being treated like shit. I made up my mind that at least one of the black players on Dallas was going to get the same financial treatment that management was giving to the white players. I went for it, demanding that my contract be renegotiated before the season began.

From the response that followed, you would have thought that I had broken some sacred law. There were stories in the press saying that I was selfish, egotistical, and worse. Gil Brandt and Tex Schramm started out with a squeeze play. The renegotiation talks were never conducted seriously—the whole thing was just dragging on.

In my time with the Cowboys I had seen that it was not unusual for guys to renegotiate their contracts. We had guys renegotiate every year. I know of one guy who renegotiated five years in a row. For the company men, the ones who were part of the establishment—somehow it was easier for them to present their ideas for renegotiation and be taken seriously.

I knew what I meant to the team at that time. The Cowboys didn't have anyone else who could do what I could, and that gave me some leverage. I realized what I brought to the whole scenario of big business: high revenue, super profits, team identity and performance. And I realized that if it took playing hardball to get what I wanted, then I would play hardball.

When training camp for the 1985 season started in Thousand Oaks, California, I wasn't there. I told Dallas management that I wouldn't be there unless I got things resolved to my satisfaction. They had their choices: negotiate with me, trade me, or do nothing.

Tom Landry was so taken aback by my holdout that it seemed he couldn't even say my name. *"His* job," Tom told the press, "and *his* responsibility is to be here. I have done everything I can for *the running back."*

Tex Schramm spoke about my being able to see the light. I wondered what light he had in mind: neon lights, bright lights, dim lights, "Randy White lights?" I didn't know the answer to those questions, but I wanted to know. What I *did* know was that I was making less money than a defensive tackle.

All kinds of quotes appeared in the newspapers attributed to Tex Schramm—a guy who always knew how to use the media to his advantage. In the *Dallas Morning News,* Tex was quoted as saying that he was willing to change my contract "in structure to resemble that of Randy White's $6.4 million annuities type deal." But privately I was told by Tex that a clause in my 1980 contract made it clear that I could not renegotiate.

There was another line in the newspapers attributed to Tex: "I've always been interested in helping Tony restructure his financial stability so that he can leave football with pride and financial stability."

The public stuff sounded good and was one thing; the private "inside" ploys were another thing, and they were insidious.

One of the ploys was related to my troubles with the IRS at that time. However, no one knew about those problems except for Tex and other people with Dallas.

All of a sudden, the IRS got bombarded with phone calls about me from the media. All that shit found its way into the newspapers. It was a cheap shot by the Cowboys, who released my entire financial situation to the press. And the way the situation was presented, it seemed that I was holding out to renegotiate my contract because of the troubles with the IRS. That was bullshit. One thing, as I said, had nothing to do with the other.

The coverage was also distorted and sensationalistic. Stories said I was bankrupt, that I lost houses, cars, this and that. It was a great example of how the media distort facts and try to make a black guy look bad. Sure, I was hurting financially, but I wasn't bankrupt. I even bought a brand-new Porsche. I wasn't missing a beat. I still had houses, cars, everything I wanted.

On his KLRD radio show, Tex Schramm mentioned that I hadn't reported to training camp because I had personal financial problems. He spread my financial affairs all over town, leaked private information about me to the media, thinking it would make me come out of the cold and report to training camp. All that did was piss me off even more and make me even more determined not to go in.

Fined each day for staying out, racked by the IRS, ripped in the newspapers—even that weasel Skip Bayless got his licks in, calling me "The Former Crown Prince of Dallas and His Indebtedness"—with all that shit going on, I still stuck to my guns. They even tried to rub it in a little more by replacing my picture on the cover of the Cowboy media guide with a picture of Randy White. That was laughable.

I issued a statement that I was prepared to sit out as long as I had to in order to get a new deal. And I was.

Another ploy used by Dallas management during my holdout was to make Ron Springs the starting halfback.

When they asked me what I thought about that, I said, "Great, I'm happy for Ron Springs. But I'm not worried about him or anyone else taking my job away from me if I want the job."

I was somewhat surprised about their putting Ron in there because Tom Landry never really appreciated Ron. A guy who kept everybody loose on the team, who was always kidding around, Ron was not Tom's kind of guy. To Tom, you've got to be serious to play football; man, if you're not serious you can't play football. Ron was not serious. It wasn't a part of his nature, but when it came time to play—he was there.

Ron was a good friend of mine, maybe my best friend on the Cowboys, but he wound up getting caught in that cross fire between Dallas management and me. All through that holdout, they thought that Ron was a middleman and had something to do with my not being there.

I remember Tex Schramm telling me, "This Ron Springs is really not a good friend of yours. He's going around telling reporters, 'Tony is not coming back. He'll stay away for ninety-nine years if he doesn't get his contract the way he wants it to be.' "

When I heard that, I called Ron up and told him, "Ron, I think the Cowboys are a little teed off at some of the things you've said. Just don't say another thing, man. I appreciate your being on my side, but I think it's working to your disadvantage."

I held out for twenty-one days, and finally we got the deal done, and I reported to camp. I got a twenty-year annuity worth six million dollars and some other good things, and I was happy about that. But the whole mess shouldn't have had to come to all that name-calling and bitterness.

A sorry postscript to the affair was that when I came back in, Ron Springs was released. It was an incredible move—a guy going from being a starting halfback to being cut. Ron's release shocked the entire team. No one could believe management would do that—not to a guy with Ron's versatility, not to a player with all that ability. But what he could do and what he had done to help the Cowboys didn't seem to matter.

We understood. Ron was being made an example of because of his individuality and outspokenness. He didn't have any influence over me, but he did have some control over a few of the younger guys. The Cowboys' management didn't like that and they didn't want Ron around because he was his own kind of man.

Getting set for my ninth NFL season in 1985, I couldn't wait for it to start. My divorce, my financial troubles, my holdout from training camp—I had put all of those things behind me. Some people said my playing would be affected by all the stresses and strains I had been going through. But throughout my career, what happened off the field happened *off* the field. When the bell rang, I always came to play football. In 1985, I plunged myself into playing football.

Near the start of that season I reached a major milestone in my career. The date was October 13. We were playing against Pittsburgh in Dallas. I joined Walter Payton, Jim Brown, Franco Harris, O. J. Simpson, and John Riggins, becoming only the sixth back in NFL history to rush for 10,000 yards. If I had to write the script I would have written it just like that—hitting the 10,000-yard mark against the black and gold of the Steelers.

As a pro I usually didn't play all that well in Pittsburgh, but that day I had a pretty good game, rushing for 113 yards and scoring two touchdowns. The 10,000th yard came on a 19-yard sweep around left end with 6:16 left in the third period. What was touching about it all was the standing ovation from the sellout crowd of 62,932, and the

congratulations of my teammates. But even then Tom
Landry didn't show any emotion. We shook hands, and I
was given the ball, and we kept right on playing Cowboy
football.

With 5:52 left to play in the game, I kind of capped my
day off. I was out in the open running and the Steelers
tried to herd me in. At that point I cut back across the
field and gave the guys chasing me my little "hello—
goodbye" move. I ran 35 yards and scored my second
touchdown, and we beat Pittsburgh 27–13.

Gaining those 10,000 yards was something I took a
great deal of pride in. It seemed that at times other backs
were getting a lot more headlines than I was and that I
was being taken for granted by some people. Yet there I
was in my ninth season—the sixth all-time rusher. Reach-
ing that level showed what kind of a runner I was,
showed my longevity and my durability, showed my ca-
pacity to take a pounding year in and year out and still
come back for more.

We came up against the New York Giants needing a
win to clinch the division title that year. There was a
drive in that game that stacks up as one of the most satisfying of my career. Maybe it was because it was at a time
the Cowboys needed a maximum effort by me most of all.
Danny White and Gary Hogeboom were both out with
injuries, and the inexperienced Steve Pelluer was in at
quarterback in the fourth quarter of that game. We
marched 72 yards for a touchdown and wound up beating
the Giants. I carried the ball four times for 40 yards and
had one catch in that drive—the biggest drive of the season.

Although we beat the Giants and the Cowboys re-
corded their thirteenth divisional title, we couldn't get
past the L.A. Rams in the first round of the playoffs. Their
defense was tough. We lost the game 20–0.

That 1985 season I rushed for 1,307 yards, scored seven touchdowns, and became the all-time leader in that department for the Cowboys with 79. Through 1985 I had 44 games of 100 yards or more rushing—and the Cowboys won 41 of those. I also had the record for the most yards rushing in Dallas playoff history, and was second behind Franco Harris on the all-time list in yards rushing in NFL playoff games.

The 1985 season ended a little earlier than we wanted it to. But I felt good that all my personal problems and the strife of the past year were history. I knew I was still at the top of my game and looked ahead to 1986 and to fulfilling Tom Landry's words: "Our offense still revolves around Tony Dorsett."

VII
GOODBYE
DALLAS

ON AUGUST 13, 1986, THE DALLAS COWBOYS AN-
nounced that they had signed Herschel Walker, the former Heisman Trophy winner out of the University of
Georgia, the former United States Football League star.

I told reporters, "The guy is an awesome talent and an
awesome physical specimen. He's big and fast, and playing in the same backfield with him will be interesting."

Those words were not just for media hype. The year
before, I had accounted for 75 percent of the Cowboys'
rushing yards on 66 percent of the team's rushing plays. I
was genuinely elated about the thought of us being in the
same backfield and spreading the work load. I thought
the two of us could be outstanding together, and I personally welcomed Herschel with open arms.

Then I learned that he was going to be paid $5 million
for five years—making him the highest-paid player on the
Cowboys. I was furious.

I got a lot of headlines when I said that I didn't know
what the salary structure was in the USFL, where Herschel came from, but I did know what the salary structure
was in Dallas. And I added that I didn't consider myself
second to any back on the Cowboys and wouldn't accept
being paid less money than any other back on the team.

To me, it didn't make any sense. They signed Herschel

Walker for all that money and he hadn't contributed one
yard to the success of the Cowboys. I got a lot more head-
lines when I said, "What's Herschel Walker ever done?
Won the Heisman Trophy? Well, I've got one of those.
He's got 2,400 yards rushing in the United States Football
League. Well, I guess he's got me there."

I was so infuriated and disgusted by the whole thing,
so annoyed by it all, that I was ready to walk out of
training camp. Then I met with Coach Landry, and he
sold me a bill of goods—that he had big plans for Herschel and me, that I'd still be the number one tailback,
that Walker and I would be great together, and that
they'd work things out. That ended the whole thing as far
as I was concerned.

The media made a big deal about the Tony Dorsett–
Herschel Walker controversy. Man, they sure had a lot to
write about. Every day there was another story, another
opinion. The whole thing, though, had nothing to do with
Herschel. I had no hard feelings toward him as a person.
We liked each other a lot right from the start and became
friends. He had nothing to do with the decisions that
were made there.

They called it the "Dream Backfield." But as things
turned out, it would become more like the "Bad Dream
Backfield." When the 1986 season began, I remained the
primary tailback. Herschel was played at fullback, in the
slot, as a motion man, at wide receiver, even at tight end.
But there was never really the "Dream Backfield." Herschel and I rarely played in a conventional tailback-full-
back setup.

Yet it could've worked with the two of us in the backfield if the Cowboys wanted it to work. The more I think
of it, the more I realize they didn't want it to work. Supposedly in Dallas they have some of the best minds in

football. Why couldn't they have come up with something? The answer is they didn't want to.

What I'll never understand is why the coaches
wouldn't take the blame for what went wrong with the
"Dream Backfield." They always had a way of putting it
off on the players. I think that Coach Landry gave up on
the idea of running me and Herschel before we ever had
a chance to really get it going. But then again, Coach
Landry never liked to take the blame.

Eugene Lockhart said, "The problem was that there
was a lot of selfishness between some of the people involved—I won't go into any names. But if they had
wanted it to work—it could have worked. Our best offense was when both Tony and Herschel were in the
game."

That 1986 season was unfortunate for me also in that I
was never 100 percent physically. With three games
missed because of a knee injury, my streak of 94 straight
starts ended. I did manage to rush for 748 yards, leading
the Cowboys again in that category, but it was the first
time in my career that I didn't rush for over 1,000 yards
when I played a full season. At the end of the year I was
in fourth place on the all-time rushing list—541 yards behind Franco Harris. And when the season ended, the
Cowboys, with a 7–9 record, missed the playoffs.

It was our first losing season in twenty years. The
handwriting was there for all to see. Dallas was more a
team of the past than ever.

The 1987 National Football League season will always
be remembered as the time of the bitter players' strike.
But I will always remember that season as the time I was
thirty-three years old and wore No. 33 as a member of the
Dallas Cowboys for the last time.

I had a strong feeling for the situation even though I

had very little to gain personally by going out on strike. With more than a decade in the league and just a couple of years of playing time left, I could easily have taken a back seat in the whole thing. But that was never my way. And as usual, I found myself in the middle of a whole lot of controversy.

On the first day of the strike, Randy White crossed the picket line. I thought he made the wrong decision. Randy is one of the more popular players in the league, and he comes from a strong union state—Delaware. In his day he was one of the best linemen in the game, he played all out, played his head off. So I felt, from a strength stand-point, he would be a valuable person to get to support the strike. But he didn't even give it one day.

Out there walking the line with a lot of other guys, seeing Randy cross—I got pissed off. I just happened to call him "Captain Scab." Some other guys called him that too. And a lot of other people called him names that were a lot worse.

But I got caught with that "Captain Scab" remark—I guess it made for good copy, because a lot of mileage was gotten out of it.

Randy White said, "I don't have a grudge against Tony. It won't be a problem. We will still be teammates trying to win games on the field. We just probably will never be the best of buddies off the field."

I was upset with Randy at that time. And I'm not apologizing for anything I said. I didn't think I had a need to talk to him. If he thought the statements I made were so strong that the little relationship we had was destroyed, so be it.

Hell, I was willing to risk my salary like everyone else. I lost $31,000 for being out one week. I had no problem with that. I was out there because I supported the union.

Then I received a letter from Tex Schramm that informed me that if I didn't stop striking and return and play in the replacement games, I would lose my annuity. That package came to millions of dollars.

Tex Schramm said, "We sent the letter because I felt some players were not advised by their agents of the situation. I didn't want them to all of a sudden realize they were jeopardizing their futures. Too many guys get a big contract at the time of signing and don't pay attention to details."

I didn't have much time to get legal counsel to react to Tex's letter. I guess you could say I was tricked or trapped by Tex Schramm. The whole thing was an unfair labor practice.

I was out on strike because I valued unions and was doing what I thought was right. But sacrificing my long-range financial security was another thing. When it came to that I had no choice but to go back in. For me to cross the ranks—yes, it was sort of contradictory, but when you look at the whole picture, anybody in America would've probably made the same decision. If that scenario had developed in the early part of my career, my decision would probably have been to stay out. But I was now at the end of my career, with no chance to make up the money Tex was telling me that I was going to lose.

That period was the weirdest in my life. First I was one of the militant union spearheads. Then I walked through the line with egg on my face. I hated it. I hated being there, hated the games I had to dress for. Physically I was on the field, but mentally I was a zillion miles away. There were all those years I took pride in wearing the silver and blue. But at that time I hated being a Dallas Cowboy. In a scab game against the Philadelphia Eagles I ran for a 10-yard touchdown and was booed by the fans. That was one of the few times I was ever booed in Texas Stadium.

When the strike was finally ended, I wondered what was accomplished. Nothing, really, except for a lot of players losing a lot of money. It was all for naught. There was all that bitterness around, lots of recriminations. The way Tex Schramm pushed management's points throughout that strike made him a hated man around the league. The way Tex acted drew a lot of hostility toward the Dallas Cowboys.

With things back to normal, Herschel and I started in the Cowboy backfield. They moved him from fullback to tailback to wideout. By mid-season I had more carries than Herschel in nonstrike games.

Then on November 15, in a game against the New England Patriots, for the first time since I had won the starting job eleven years before, I didn't start at tailback. I got into the game for only six plays, carried the ball only once, while Herschel carried the ball twenty-eight times.

There was an awful lot I didn't like about that, especially the way I was treated. None of the coaches were men enough to come up to me and tell me what the hell was going on. None of them had the guts to tell me that Herschel was going to start that game. The only way I knew about it was to hear it through the media. Shit, that was a blow! It was then that I decided that if this was the way things were going to be, I wanted out!

Tom Landry said that he could feel for me in that situation. "It's hard for a player to be the number one focal point of an offense for so many years," he said, "and all of a sudden someone else comes along and either shares that role or seems to be the replacement for him. Not too many athletes can handle that without frustration. I don't know any that could."

For me the whole thing was not so much frustration as a matter of pride. I knew I hadn't lost a step or one bit of my ability. All that was happening was that they were messing with my talent and my head.

I could appreciate that the Cowboys were in transition, trying to get some new blood in there and prepare for the future. I had no qualms about that. But it couldn't be denied that I was one of the best offensive weapons they had. If I wasn't the best, then I was pretty damn close to it.

How do you just take away that kind of weapon from your offense? How can a coach, in the space of one week, say one star running back is as good as the other and then cut one of them out? How can you go, in the space of one week, from being great to being chopped liver?

You work for greatness. One week I was running as well as I ever had in my career, looking as good as I ever had. And the next week it was like I was nothing. Nobody had anything to say to me. It was like hey, man, you're not good enough to step out on the field anymore. I couldn't understand it. The majority of the players on the team couldn't understand how I could put up with it.

As far as Herschel Walker goes, I don't have an envious bone in my body toward him. I hope he has a great career in Dallas. We're friends.

Herschel and his wife came over for Thanksgiving dinner in 1987, and my mother was there too, bothered by the turn of events. She was so upset that she told me she even rehearsed a little speech that she was going to deliver to Herschel.

When Herschel stepped into the house, he held out a nice basket of flowers. "Mrs. Dorsett," he said, "I brought these for you."

That gesture got to my mom and showed her that Herschel was not a part of the problem, but she was still angry about what she called my playing "second fiddle."

In the ninth game of the 1987 season, I didn't fiddle at

all. We played Miami. No. Dallas played Miami. I was
DNP. Did Not Play!

I was the guy with the clean jersey. The other guys on
the Cowboys, the veterans especially, they just stared at
the ground. They all realized if it could happen to Tony
Dorsett, it could happen to anyone.

Tom Landry claimed that he had designed an offense
that probably could've worked with both Herschel and
me. That was what he claimed. "By sharing the load and
using the different types of offense," Coach Landry said,
"Tony would have still gotten the yardage. However, he
got to the point where he wanted me to make a decision
—to have one tailback or the other. And of course I made
the decision at that time that I needed to go with Herschel. We were rebuilding the team and we couldn't have
an offense that was compatible to everybody."

What Tom was saying was that I could have hung on
with Dallas and sat on the stool and milked the cow and
picked up the cash. But that was never my way.

And their way is what still ticks me off. The way I was
treated was like meat on the hoof. They didn't care—it
was like, "Man, you've had your years." They didn't give
a damn. They used me up and now to hell with me. It was
pure meanness.

I was bitter, mad, frustrated, but under control.

Normally, going through that kind of shit I would have
exploded more than once. But they had their plan—and I
had my plan.

I told Tex Schramm, "I want out." I told Tom Landry, "I
want to be traded!" They gave me that old bullshit story,
that song-and-dance routine that they would try to ac-
commodate me.

The other players on the team realized that if they
could do this to me, shit, they could do it to any of them. I
am sure that what happened to me enlightened all the

players in Dallas about what the business of pro football
is all about. And if some of the players on the Cowboys
didn't like me as a person, they at least respected me for
what I brought to the team as an athlete, for what I
brought to the picnic.

I told them, "Get what you can get, know your value,
know what you're worth. Don't let them bullshit you. Get
what you can get and get out."

I wasn't going to end my career wasting away with the
Dallas Cowboys. They chose not to use me, and that was
not a situation I could tolerate.

Tom Landry said, "That's the evolution of football.
Guys have great careers. They come to the end of their
careers where they have only a few more years left. And
you have a great young guy replacing them. It's an endless thing you go through in this business. It's always sad
because you have to put somebody down who has meant
so much to your football team and your success through
the years."

But what still rankles me is that going into the 1987
season I needed just 733 yards to pass Jim Brown and
become the number two rusher of all time. And I was
given the opportunity to carry the ball just 130 times that
year. I remember how it felt not being able to play or
being used very sparingly. Running in and out of games
isn't my style. I was put in a role so limited that I couldn't
stand it—and I couldn't understand it.

Coach Landry and management knew how close I was
to passing Jim Brown and yet they wouldn't put me out on
the field to do it. It sure wouldn't have taken a lot, but
they just refused to let it happen. I finished the 1987 season in Dallas still needing 426 yards to pass Jim Brown; it
was almost as if Jim Brown was gaining on me rather
than the other way around.

"Sure, Tony could've caught a couple of guys," Coach

Landry said. "But what more could Tony achieve than he already accomplished?"

One of the more touching things that happened when it was clear that I was determined to leave the Cowboys was all the letters I received. They came from all over the country from people who had followed my career. Most of the letters urged me not to leave the Cowboys and there were quite a few that wondered why Dallas management had treated me the way it had.

Considering the roller-coaster career I had in Dallas, considering the controversial figure I was, it really got to me reading all those letters from all those people who cared.

That last game for me in Texas Stadium as a Dallas Cowboy was just that—my last game, just a normal game. I wasn't feeling well enough to play, but I wasn't in the right frame of mind to play anyway, considering the way things were going.

I really didn't feel any special emotion. I knew it was the last time I'd wear a Dallas Cowboy uniform and that it was the end of something that I was a part of for eleven seasons . . . Maybe I thought that some part of me would always be in the franchise, some part of me would always be on the Dallas Cowboys, but I really don't remember that day very well.

Cast in such a limited role, I finished the 1987 season, the second losing season in a row for the Cowboys, with the fewest carries of my career, the fewest yards gained, the fewest yards per carry, the fewest touchdowns.

For the first time in my career, a back other than Tony Dorsett led Dallas in rushing. It was a real downer. I think the Cowboys owed me something more than that after all those years. Dallas prides itself on being a class organization. But in my case there was no class at all.

I was being paid by them, so I guess they felt they

could do anything they wanted. But I gave them more than just running and catching. I gave them not only my body but also my heart and soul.

Once I put a football suit on, once I strapped on my headgear, I could always be depended on to do the things I had to do. That was always the main thing. I could always be counted on to do my job—I gave it everything I had.

After all I gave, I felt I deserved more respect. It was upsetting to feel I was getting screwed by the Cowboys. Forget the 12,000-plus yards that I rushed for, forget the eight 1,000-yard seasons, the 46 100-yard games that I racked up when the Cowboys came up with a 42–4 record, forget the way I helped them win championship games, the way I played in two Super Bowls.

Forget even that in eleven seasons with the Cowboys I missed very few games, three or four, not many considering my size and the injuries I picked up. I was ready, always ready, to play, week in and week out. There were lots of times that I could easily have said I couldn't play, but I never did that. When it mattered a great deal, I played. When it didn't matter at all, I played. With pain, with cracked ribs three years in a row, with broken toes and fingers, knee problems, I played. You name the injury —I was still out there. Sometimes I was nauseous or my head was pounding or my knees were killing me, but I had that work ethic and that responsibility to the Dallas Cowboys and I played.

But even forgetting all that, they still had to take note that I was Tony Dorsett, a guy who played a major role in their tradition down there, a guy who was responsible for a lot of what the Dallas Cowboys accomplished. Maybe they took note, but they didn't give a damn.

Tom Landry did not run me out of town. Cowboy president Tex Schramm did not run me out of town. Not play-

ing me ran me out of town. They chose not to use me and
that was something I wouldn't stand for.

Not everything I did in Dallas was accepted by the
people who ran the team. Not everything they did was
accepted by me. Sometimes I felt like I was loved, but not
all the time. As I said, somebody once called me "the
love-hate back." That was a pretty close description.

There was the reputation, the image, of my being a
troublemaker. That wasn't accurate. I didn't make trouble, but I never backed away from it either. And I had to
live with that too. That was a bad feeling, being in a city I
loved, playing for a great organization, going through a
lot . . . and having the feeling there were people against
me. That hurt a lot.

During the 1988 off-season trade rumors about me were
everywhere. I was getting sick and tired of hearing them.
I wanted out of Dallas badly. Spring of 1988 rolled around
and still nothing had happened.

In May at the mini-camp the team was running some
drills. I went to Daryl Clack, one of the young guys on the
Cowboys. "I'm not planning on being here, Daryl," I told
him. "You run the drills. Get yourself ready."

Later reporters came over to me and asked why I had
not run any of the drills. I told them that I was mentally
exhausted and just didn't feel like doing any running.

The press made a bigger deal over that than it was.
Frank Luksa wrote in the *Dallas Times Herald:* "What
the Cowboys could always depend on with Dorsett—he
would go to war for them—had disappeared. Here was a
problem with only one solution. He had to go."

Sure, what I had done was uncharacteristic behavior,
but no one came to me and asked me to participate in the
drills. I wasn't planning to do anything to upset the Cowboys, but my not running surely alerted them to how seriously I wanted out. But they also knew that anytime I

stepped out on that field as long as I was a member of that team they could count on me putting forth my best effort. That would never change. I can't ever afford to go out there and not try my best. It's a violent game, and I'm not going to go out there bullshitting with my health and my life at stake.

I'm not writing this book to take any unfair shots at the Dallas Cowboys. Shit, I had a great career there. Even in my last season, with the strike and all and the limited playing time, I still reached a few more personal milestones. I became only the fourth player in NFL history to rush for more than 12,000 yards. I also moved into second place behind Walter Payton on the NFL's all-time combined yards list.

It's funny how life goes in circles. Back when I was at Pitt and thinking of a pro career, I dreamed of playing for the Pittsburgh Steelers. Now, more than a decade later, I was thinking of playing for the black and gold again. I would have enjoyed coming home and finishing my career in the city where it all began.

But unfortunately Coach Chuck Noll probably thought I'd play for three years and he'd have to pay me for forty. He didn't want to take on that kind of financial situation.

On Monday, June 6, 1988, I was traded to the Denver Broncos. They were at the top of the list for me. I knew Dan Reeves, their head coach, from my early years in Dallas. I knew the Denver system, and I felt the adjustment on the field was not going to be that big a deal for me.

Interestingly enough, it was Denver, not Dallas, that notified me of the trade. And just for a brief moment there my thoughts drifted back to 1977 and a phone call from Gil Brandt telling me that I was a member of the Dallas Cowboys.

When the initial excitement of the news of the trade

passed and it finally sank in that I was no longer a Dallas Cowboy, but was a Denver Bronco, when the reality of what had happened hit me, I became somewhat apprehensive. After all, after eleven seasons with the Cowboys, after all that time of giving the team an identity, of forming so many friendships, it was strange to think of starting over with a new team. But that thinking didn't last long.

When I left Dallas I thought of how Tex Schramm used to say that "time heals all." That's how I feel. Time, I guess, will heal everything. I had a great career with Dallas. I don't hate the Cowboys. How can I? It's the team that gave Tony Dorsett all his fame and recognition. When people think of Tony Dorsett they will always think of the Dallas Cowboys.

After the trade was announced, there were all kinds of reactions from all over the place. Fans and sportswriters, relatives and friends, players and coaches, it seemed everybody had some kind of opinion. One thing it sure showed was that I was still a lightning rod.

Herschel Walker was sympathetic. "The guy gave his heart," he said. "He piled up so many yards and great moments in Texas Stadium . . . and he has to finish up his career somewhere else. It was like being pulled out of your own house."

Tex Schramm was diplomatic: "There was nothing positive in trading Tony from our standpoint. He always gave all of himself to the franchise. It's sad that someone with the contributions and history that Tony has with the Dallas Cowboys is not going to finish his career here. He's the first player of his caliber that hasn't finished his career here and continued to be a part of the Cowboys.

"But today," Tex continued, "if I want to call Herschel Walker the best running back in football, I can do that without reservation. A major distraction has been eliminated. Before, all of us had to be so careful of what we said because we didn't want to hurt the feelings of one guy or another."

Tom Landry was analytical: "It's just a difficult thing to keep people happy, but there was no way we could resolve the situation to the benefit of both parties. Our team approach was changing. We were going into the big offensive line—that means the big power runners like Herschel. Tony didn't fit that mold. I think Tony has a couple of good years left. I can't speak for him. I can only speak for myself. I miss him. I would have loved to have seen him finish his career here in Dallas. But it wasn't to be."

Danny White was angry: "I think the whole deal stunk," he said. "We are a very young team right now, younger than any team I can remember, so that makes the leadership much more important. I've seen Tony in just about any kind of situation a running back can get into and he's always responded. There's not a runner around with Tony's acceleration and deception. I haven't seen any drop-off in speed, acceleration, the other things he's known for. If anything, Tony got better with age and experience. We needed him there on the scene. What if Herschel gets hurt?"

Roger Staubach was philosophical: "For Tony's greatness as a player, he should have been a major part of the city of Dallas. It didn't happen that way, so it's a kind of good news, bad news. He had a tremendous career here, but wasn't really able to take advantage of it. Tony has meant as much to the Dallas Cowboy football team as any player in the history of the team. Not to be recognized as myself, a Bob Lilly, a Drew Pearson—it should not be that way. He's meant as much or more than any of us to the Dallas franchise. Tony is one of the truly great running backs that ever played the game. If you took the top five running backs and placed them in any order you wanted—he's right there. It's a shame that he left Dallas in circumstances that were not ideal. For a guy like Tony, his leaving should have been an event of appreciation for all he did for the Cowboys. There are only a few players like Tony that you have in a lifetime on a team.

"Tony could have said, 'Okay, I'll sit on the bench. You pay me. You play me when you want to.' But his pride and the knowledge that he had a lot left in him wouldn't let him do that.

"I wasn't coaching the team but I think they could've gotten both Walker and Dorsett in the game. I just don't think the whole situation was handled very well."

When my playing days are over, I'll go to the games at Texas Stadium if they let me continue to buy my season tickets. You never know . . . but bumming tickets is definitely not my style. I'm a Dallas Cowboy fan. That won't ever change. Regardless of what I think of certain individuals, they're not the team.

Some people have asked me if I think I'll ever get admitted to the Ring of Honor. It's something that adds to the mystique of the team and is the Dallas Cowboy version of the Hall of Fame. A player who qualifies has his name placed on the Ring that runs around Texas Stadium. There's a big ceremony at halftime of a game in which the player admitted to the Ring of Honor gets to ride around Texas Stadium in a car with his family. It's a nice deal and they always do it up in style.

A lot of great players who have starred for the Cowboys have been taken into the Ring of Honor: Bob Lilly, Roger Staubach, Don Meredith, Don Perkins, Chuck Howley, Mel Renfro. But a lot of other great players haven't been admitted. Lee Roy Jordan is not there. Bob Hayes is not in. I don't know what it takes to qualify for the Ring of Honor. Do you have to be the right kind of player? Do you have to be a great player?

Admission to the Ring is through committee choice. It was always a one-man committee—Tex Schramm. The Ring was his personal baby. If Tex decided he wanted somebody there—up he went into the Ring.

I don't know if I'll ever be admitted to the Ring of Honor. If I am, fine. If not, then that's fine too. With all the success I had with the Dallas Cowboys, I feel I deserve to be put up there in the Ring. Will I be? Who knows?

But I've put the Dallas Cowboys behind me. When I left the team all I took was my helmet, my jersey, and the pads I wore. I was never one to clutter my house or cars with a lot of junk or a bunch of team paraphernalia like a lot of guys do. I moved on to new horizons. There is no bad blood. I have my memories and that's more than enough.

VIII
HELLO
DENVER

A LOT OF PEOPLE MADE A BIG FUSS OUT OF THE fact that when I was traded to Denver I was thirty-four years old. They went into the old sunset stories of Franco Harris hanging on at the end of his career with the Seattle Seahawks and Earl Campbell creaking along with the New Orleans Saints. They brought up stories of O. J. Anderson with nothing left still trying to play for the New York Giants, and O. J. Simpson, a sorry shadow of what he once was, picking up paychecks with the San Francisco 49ers.

But I knew all football players were different individuals. I wasn't Earl Campbell or Franco Harris. And I knew that neither of the O.J.s ever ran a 4.38 40 yards at age thirty-four. I knew that if I could have been put on a track for a sprint with any of those guys when we were all thirty-four-year-olds, I would have burned them off.

I thought of myself as a guy who had aged more gracefully than other running backs. I looked at myself as a fine wine that Denver just pulled off the rack in the wine cellar.

Yet, coming into Denver, I admit I was a little apprehensive about a newspaper poll that was taken as to who the fans wanted—George Rogers or me. I lost out in that poll by a landslide. So I was wondering how I was going to be received and perceived. I didn't see myself as coming out to Colorado and being a savior or a quick fix. I didn't see myself as being one of the leaders there. Denver had plenty of leaders. All I was looking forward to was being one of the guys and just fitting in. Of course, I had high expectations for myself. I've always had them and always will. And now I was looking forward to playing for Denver and finishing out my career playing as well as I knew I could.

Any apprehensions I had about how I was going to be accepted were quickly dispelled by the wonderful reception I received. The Chamber of Commerce hosted a dinner for me when I first arrived. The fans were friendly and warm. Coming into Denver was a great experience for me. It was a different environment and a different franchise, and it was stimulating for me to discover that things could be just as good if not better than in Dallas. The whole scenario was very refreshing.

Denver is beautiful. The only thing that was a bit unsettling was the height of those Rocky Mountains. I always knew I had a problem with height. Glass elevators, open balconies, being in a room high up in a tall building —all those things always bothered me. When I first got to Denver I made the mistake of taking a ride up into the mountains and it just freaked me out. I'm not a mountain man. The Rockies are scenic and all that, but I'll leave them to the skiers and hikers. But I do love the air and the flowers and trees in Denver. I also like the people associated with the football franchise.

In Dallas it was all about intimidation. It was "Ooooh, ooooh, I'm going to scare you today, buddy." Tom Landry, Tex Schramm—those guys never made you feel very good.

I was reminded of how intimidating and cold the Dallas organization could be when I received reports about the fan mail and phone calls the Cowboys got after I left. People who cared about me called up and got "Hey, he doesn't work here anymore. Don't call us up. He's not a Dallas Cowboy." I know that once you're gone from the Cowboys—unless you're Roger Staubach or someone like that—you're no longer part of their thinking. But hell, you'd think that after all I did for that franchise, they would be less abrupt with people who wanted to reach out to me.

In Denver, the people in charge made me feel very good right from the start. I like being able to have a chance to go in and joke with the coaches, to talk to the owner one-on-one. And that's what I was able to do in Denver. In a way, for me it was like being a kid growing up in Aliquippa, afraid to try something new. I was that way for a while—used to Dallas, afraid to try something new. Now I've discovered that there is more to the NFL than Dallas. There are situations you can be in—like Denver—that are just as good if not better.

The Bronco owner, Pat Bowlen, is always there. He'll come to practice and chitchat with the players. Although he has a lot of clout and calls the shots and signs the checks, he's not the kind of man you feel intimidated by. Pat is a warm, open guy, someone you can sit down with and talk to.

Right off the bat when I arrived in Denver, I had dinner with Dan Reeves. We talked football for a while and it was exciting for me. Sitting there with Dan in the restaurant, I thought that through all those years in Dallas, not once did I ever get the chance to sit down with Tom Landry over dinner and talk football with him.

Dan Reeves is the kind of coach that you respect and want to work hard for. He's dedicated to winning, but at the same time he tells jokes and treats players like men.

It seems funny that Landry was the teacher and Reeves was his student. But lately the student had more success.

One of the ways Dan is a lot different from Tom Landry as a coach is that he gives his players much more freedom. At the training camp it is possible to leave on weekends or even during the week and drive back into the city. Your family is allowed to come up to the training camp and eat dinner with you and spend a night there. Beer is served on Wednesday nights. All of these things break the monotony, the grueling routine of an NFL training camp. All the players appreciate things like that.

The whole Denver experience proved to be a good working environment. During the season lunch was catered on Fridays and the players looked forward to that change of pace. Also, we never ran sprints the way we did in Dallas, and I especially liked that. I believe that you can burn an athlete out as the season progresses, after all the hitting and physical abuse to his body, and if you have to keep running those sprints, it tears you down. That's what happened in Dallas; so not to have to go through it was something I really appreciated.

When I first got to Denver there was stuff in the papers about my getting No. 33. Gene Lang had worn that number for the Broncos, but it was also synonymous with me throughout my career. That number came about through my older brothers. It was a family thing. When they first started playing football in junior high school and high school they wore No. 21. That vanished and they got No. 24. Then when that vanished, they went to No. 33. My brother Keith started with No. 33, and then I began wearing it in junior high school and high school. I've been wearing it ever since. But it's no big deal—I've never been caught up with the number. Dan Reeves and management said that No. 33 was something they wanted me to have. I got my old number, but I could have taken it or left it, especially if it was going to create problems. But I guess to a lot of people I looked weird enough being in a different uniform. I would have looked even more out of place wearing a different number.

Being in Denver after all the years with the Cowboys, being around different people, different training facilities —that was all weird. And when I put on the Denver Bronco uniform for the first time in a game, that's when it really hit me. It was strange going from the silver and blue to the orange and blue, but although the costume was different, it was the same me inside.

The season itself was one of highs and lows for me. Early on I scored my first touchdown as a Bronco on a 21-yard run that John Elway kiddingly called a "34-year-old burst." I didn't care what they called it. Scoring that TD felt pretty good and helped move me a little further up the all-time yardage ladder.

Then on September 12, 1988, on a six-yard gain in a game against the San Diego Chargers, I went past Franco Harris into the number three spot on the all-time rushing list. I picked up 113 yards in that game.

Now I was looking for Jim Brown. On September 27, 1988, I found him in a Monday-night game we played against the Los Angeles Raiders. The game went into overtime, and we wound up suffering a frustrating 30–27 loss. Somewhere in the overtime I caught and passed Jim Brown on a six-yard run to the Raider side of the field. I got up not really knowing for sure if I had surpassed him or not.

The plan was to stop the game and have a little ceremony when I made my move into second place on the all-time list. But what with the overtime, the tight game, the fact that surpassing the mark didn't take place on a pretty good run—we just let it pass. Passing Jim Brown was more meaningful to me than a ceremony anyway, more meaningful than keeping the football. Maybe if I had passed Jim with a flashy run, a long run, a Tony Dorsett-type run, I would have kept the ball.

When I passed him, no doubt some of the glamour and glory that should have been there wasn't. That was because it was something that should have been done a year before, but the Cowboys didn't give me the chance to do it.

But passing Jim Brown was something I was looking forward to doing, something I knew was going to happen —unless I came to find myself involved in some catastrophe.

Moving past Franco Harris into third place and especially going past Jim Brown into second place on the all-time rushing list are major milestones in my career. Catching them is something that I will cherish for years to come. Yet I'll always feel somewhat bittersweet about the accomplishments because they should have come in a Dallas Cowboy uniform a year earlier.

When I was at the University of Pittsburgh, Franco Harris was on the Pittsburgh Steelers. I was a Steeler fan, but I was never a Franco Harris fan. I never liked his style of running. A lot of people questioned Franco's toughness, his going out of bounds and stuff like that. That was a rap against him. I've gone out of bounds too at times during my career, but I wasn't Franco's size. Yet that was Franco's personality, and I guess there's always going to be something someone can criticize you for. Franco had a lot of success in the NFL. I saw him rip us apart as a runner in Dallas. I admired his talent and liked him as a person, but, as I said, I was never a big fan of his running style.

The guys I especially looked forward to surpassing in total career yards gained were O.J. and Jim Brown. When you talk of running backs all the comparisons are made to Jim Brown. He's the immortal. I've seen him run on film, and although he played so long ago, I do believe that he's one of the few guys from his era who could still excel today.

Jim gained 12,312 yards in just 118 games and accomplished in nine years what it's taken others ten or eleven or twelve years, sixteen games a year, to do. Just think how many yards he would have had if he had continued to play only two more years. A big, strong, fast runner—Jim Brown was the prototype back. Everything got patterned after Jim Brown. Everyone was compared to Jim Brown. He set the standards.

To have passed the immortal Jim Brown is something I'll always cherish because I consider him the greatest runner ever. As the years go on, everybody may still be trying to catch Walter Payton, because he's number one as the all-time rusher, but Jim Brown's name is always going to come up because he gained so many yards in so few years.

I rank Walter Payton extremely high among the runners that I've seen in modern-day football. I admired his toughness, competitiveness, durability. Walter was a complete back who could run, catch the ball, block.

Although Walter never possessed great speed, was never known for his speed, he could go the distance. If you had a good angle on him, you could run him down, but you can run anybody down with the right angle. He was not a real big back, but he would attack and be physical if he had to. His style of running—carrying the ball with one hand and doing a little stutter step—meant so much to the NFL.

It was nice to see Walter finally get into the Super Bowl, but I would have liked to see him score a touchdown. The Bears would get so close and then let the Refrigerator or somebody else carry it in. I've always thought that was too bad.

I watched O. J. Simpson run against the Steelers in Pittsburgh once when I was in college. He was such a smooth runner, a graceful tailback, one of the most elusive runners I've ever seen. I liked him a lot. O.J. could also catch the ball and pass-block, and his cuts and speed were outstanding. In his time O.J. was like the Dr. J. of football, an ambassador for the NFL, a very charming and likable guy. He brought a lot to the game and meant a lot to the game.

I never dreamed early in my career that I'd move past O.J. on the all-time rushing list, not to mention Jim Brown, Franco Harris, and John Riggins. When I passed Franco and Riggins, those weren't such special moments, though. It's nothing against Franco or Riggins, or even a guy like Larry Csonka for that matter. They all had great careers and did big things for their teams. But they were bulldog-type runners who didn't excite many people. Just running into guys looking for contact gets the job done, but that type of running is not very pretty. It's running ugly.

I look at John Riggins the way I do Joe Frazier. He was one of those backs whose style was not very memorable. Yeah, he got the tough yards, but today there are backs who get the tough yards but get them in a graceful way. They can do things that your grandma can appreciate instead of running straight ahead all the time.

I started off the season with the Broncos getting my hands on the ball a lot, and in the first three to five weeks I was among the top rushers in the AFC. I turned in two 100-yard efforts in the Broncos' first four games. It looked like I had the possibility of a Pro Bowl type of year if I kept getting my hands on the football. But that didn't happen. After my fifth week, my usage dwindled dramatically.

Lots of thoughts went through my mind. I spoke to some of the coaches about it, and they told me that they would have liked me to have the ball in my arms more but they were not calling the shots. Then I went in to talk to Dan Reeves to get a reading of the situation.

"Is something the matter?" I asked. "Is there something that I'm not doing or that I can do?"

"No, Tony," he said. "We're extremely happy with you and the way you've fit in. Your teammates accept you. Everybody likes you." Then Dan explained that my lack of usage came about because of concern over our offensive line and blowouts the team had suffered.

It was encouraging to sit down with Dan and talk and learn that the reason for my not being run was not something I wasn't doing. Throughout a career people tell you all kinds of things—some being the truth, some being to hide things, some to protect or help other people. I digested all that Dan had told me, and although I thought I could bring more to the picnic and was somewhat discouraged by not getting the opportunity, I accepted what he said.

I was not playing for my ego. I had fulfilled my ego a long time ago. If I was the Tony Dorsett of past years, I could easily have flown off the handle. But at thirty-four, with the years coming down to a precious one or two, there would have been nothing in it for me. It would not have worked to my advantage; the Broncos were having a so-so year and had enough problems without my creating any more.

There were things that happened with the press last year that the Tony Dorsett of the early Dallas years would not have let pass by. I would have had something to say, and no doubt there would have been quite a bit of controversy. But I've lived and learned, and I know what my leverage is. I still can play, and play well, but I'm

winding down my career. And I'm not about to be prod-
ded into running my mouth.

Reporters would come around with silly questions like
"Can you run the football from the shotgun formation?"
That was ridiculous. People asking that kind of question
don't know football, because even in the shotgun the
quarterback still has to hand the ball off to the running
back. Ace back, the two-back set, or the shotgun—I can
play in any offense.

Then there was the issue of my blocking ability. Some
of those media people would ask, "How good a blocker
are you?" Let's face it. Man, you pay people up front for
blocking. It's their job. I'm 185 pounds and I didn't make
my bread and butter in this league blocking 255-pound
linebackers. Blocking is not my forte. My thing is running
with the football. That's my pride and joy—my claim to
fame.

The most ridiculous rumor of all—one that I'm sure sur-
faced just to sell newspapers—was that there was a
power struggle over whether the Broncos were Dorsett's
team or Elway's team.

I'm sure no one even took that seriously unless they
were crazy. There I was in my twelfth season in the
league just trying to fit in as a new member of the Broncos. John had taken Denver to two straight Super Bowls
and was the symbol of the franchise. All I wanted to do
was to contribute to a winning season.

And there were also reports and rumors that claimed
John was annoyed because the Broncos were spending
too much time trying to run the ball. John destroyed those
pretty fast.

We got along very well. He told me that he's a fan of
mine, and the feeling is mutual. I like the guy and think
he's a super talent. Although he's a family man, he's also
the kind of guy who will belly up and have a beer with

you, and John's someone I like to belly up and have a beer with.

The Broncos do not yet have the mystique the Dallas Cowboys had, but the team has earned respect for the quarterback position—John Elway's position. His will to win makes for greatness. He's proven himself with his ability to bring the team back with long drives down the field. John can win a game from anywhere on the field with his scrambling ability, his quick release, his ability to thread the needle.

Both John and Roger Staubach are a lot alike in their leadership ability and intensity. If you give him the ball with enough time on the clock, John, like Roger, feels he can always win the game.

I've seen John do some incredible things on the football field, like running the ball one way and then throwing it the other way back across his body—airing it out on the run.

John has all the tools to rewrite the record book. That is, if Dan Marino doesn't push the records up so far that they become untouchable. John is big and strong and durable. There's no one close to him today in the ability to throw a football with accuracy and velocity. We'll have to wait and see just how good he can still become, but I think he has a real shot at being the number one all-time yardage leader. John has some catching up to do, but I think he can do it.

The one area that I think he can still improve is the velocity he puts on the ball. He throws a hard ball. During training camp I was trying to catch one of his balls and it hit the tip of my baby finger and tore the tendons. I think when John starts to take a little off some of his passes, he'll be even more effective. And I'm not saying that out of pity for my twisted baby finger.

After my production was cut—I carried the ball just

three to five times a game—reporters started coming to me. "Do you think it has anything to do with the draft choice Dallas will get from Denver and your contract bonus clauses?" they asked. They pointed out that if I reached 750 yards, I would be paid $175,000 on top of my $500,000 base. They also noted that if I gained 750 yards, Denver would have to give a number three draft pick to the Cowboys.

I left all of that alone. I didn't want to get myself involved in any of that kind of thinking. I hated to believe that Dan Reeves would have given me a chance to come to Denver, to finish my career the way I wanted to, and then cut me off from my running because the Broncos were worried about draft choices or incentive clause bonuses.

I couldn't imagine that the Broncos wouldn't let me run just to save some money. I'd been around the NFL long enough to know that things like that happen, but I didn't think that was the case with Denver.

The main thing that happened in 1988 with the Broncos was that the team, in general, was sub par. None of the big stars had big years. John Elway was struggling. The offensive line was struggling and wasn't able to play with any consistency because some of the key guys got hurt. And although they enjoyed pass blocking and protecting John, the guys on the offensive line wanted to run-block too. But that didn't happen too much. We got blown out in those four or five games. Starting off in those games, being so far behind, it was obvious that the fastest way, the only way, to catch up was through the air, throwing the football. Doing that took us out of the running game.

For a back to be productive, he has to be out there on the field to get a flow, a rhythm for the game. And that wasn't happening, not for me, not for Steve Sewell, not for Sammy Winder, not for Gerald Wilhite, nor any of the other backs.

That scenario of a beat-up offensive line, of the blowouts, of guys having an off year, made the running game not much of a factor. In the last five games of the season, I had a grand total of 25 carries. Shit, I figured I'd get at least 25 carries a game when I first arrived in Denver.

As the season wound down, with the team having been in two previous Super Bowls and then being blown out, embarrassed those two or three times on national television, it was clear that something had to happen. We heard, through the rumor mill, that the defensive coordinator Joe Collier, who had been with the Broncos for many years, and some other coaches might be released.

Prior to our last game, Denver owner Pat Bowlen made some strong statements about a Bronco shakeup to the media. His words put Dan Reeves into a position where he had to clean house abruptly. The rumor mill had the scoop. Joe Collier; Craig Morton, the quarterback coach; and some of the other coaches were released. What happened underscored again the business of pro football—*winning* is the bottom line.

Nevertheless, the season could have been a lot worse for me. I could have been in a place where they had the worst record in the NFL, where they won just three games, and where they had very few fans in the stands: a place called Dallas. Mile High Stadium was sold out for every single Bronco game. People came from all over Colorado, Wyoming, Montana, Utah, and New Mexico, dressed in parkas and ski clothing getups. There'd be all that orange and blue floating around. Those fans just got beside themselves—78,000-plus—boisterous, really behind the team. I had never experienced anything like that in Dallas.

In my final game with Denver last year, despite the fact

that it had been a disappointing season, the fans all came out to show their support and their love of the Broncos. They also got behind me, yelling for me to run the ball.

I went into that game thinking that if I could get a chance to run I would show my stuff, show I still had the juice. I wanted the people to see something. Sure, I'm not the Tony Dorsett of 1977, but I know I can still run the football on a very competitive level as well or better than most backs in the National Football League.

I had a good day—10 carries, 86-plus yards, a touchdown. It was my first since the fourth game of the season when I scored twice against the Raiders. I wound up the year with 703 yards rushing on 181 carries. It could have been an even more productive day if I had gotten the ball just a little more. We were running the ball really well against the Patriots and I could feel something was about ready to pop. It kind of surprised me the way New England played because they had a chance to beat us and go into the playoffs, but we beat them 21–10. They had everything to gain, and I thought they would be more emotional. But we played the spoilers' role. And we also played for pride. You always want to end the season on a winning note and that's what we did, and we had something to build on for next year.

I ended the year running the football and playing pretty well and that was encouraging. I have no regrets about the Denver season. Sure, I wanted to win more football games and I wanted do better personally, but overall being on the Broncos was a rewarding experience for me.

Before that final game last year, I was out on the field getting loose. Jim Toomey, one of the older NFL officials, came over to me.

"Hey, Tony, quit looking in the stands. Quit looking for the girls."

"Aw, man," I said, "I'm not looking for any girls."

Then Sammy Winder, one of the Denver backs, came over. "Hey, Jim, didn't you and Dusty come into the league the same time?"

The guys on Denver call me "Dusty" for "old as dust." I don't feel old, but I know I have more to look back at in the NFL than I have waiting for me ahead. Going into my thirteenth and probably final season, I'm the oldest running back around. . . .

I'm kind of like the last of the Mohicans—outlasting all the running backs of my era: Walter Payton, Franco Harris, Earl Campbell, Billy Sims, William Andrews, Wilbert Montgomery, Wendell Tyler, Ricky Bell, Rob Carpenter, Mike Pruitt, Pete Johnson. . . . I've outlasted them all.

IX
OVERTIME

I SOMETIMES WONDER WHERE ALL THE YEARS have gone. It seems to me that it's just the blink of an eye from being in rookie camp to going out there and playing in an Old-Timers' game.

I've had my runs against Carl Eller, Jim Marshall, Alan Page and the rest of the Purple People Eaters of the Minnesota Vikings. I've gone against the Orange Crush of the Denver Broncos. I had to play against the tough men of steel: Ernie Holmes, "Mean" Joe Greene and those guys on the Pittsburgh Steelers; the Killer B's of Miami, the rough tough Raiders; Leonard Marshall, Harry Carson, Lawrence Taylor of the New York Giants; and Dave Butz, Dexter Manley, and the rest of that crew on the Washington Redskins . . . and all the others . . . I never feared any of them.

But there are a lot of them that I respect because of what they've accomplished and how they've passed the test of time.

It's a great feeling for me to have survived in this game of big men as long as I have, and to have been as productive as I have over all these long years. To have been able to mix it up with the big boys week in and week out, year in and year out—it's all been pretty amazing to me.

I outlasted all the backs of my era and the guys who

won the Heisman when I was at the University of Pittsburgh—John Cappelletti, Archie Griffin, Ricky Bell. In recent years Heisman Trophy winners have had superb careers in the NFL, but in my college time you didn't know
whether they'd make it in the league or not.

Talent is just one part of it. Once you get to the NFL
level, the mental part becomes even more important, the
burning desire, the applying of yourself, the learning
about the game. I've seen a lot of talented players over
the years, but that's all they had—talent. They didn't do
anything with it. Some were uncoachable. Others were
unresponsive, had poor work habits, no drive. Guys
would have success and try to coast along with it, and
they'd get stagnant.

John Cappelletti of Penn State won the Heisman when
I was a freshman at Pitt. He came into the NFL with a lot
of fanfare, but he didn't do anything that much in pro
ball.

Ricky Bell was picked ahead of me in the draft by
Tampa Bay and was my competition for the Heisman
Trophy award. John McKay of Tampa Bay, a team people
called "USC East," was Ricky's coach at USC and
wanted to have a big, prototype running back. Ricky was
a hard-nosed player with good speed, but I never did
think he was all that outstanding a runner. It was sad to
see him die of that rare disease.

Archie Griffin had an exceptional college career and is
the only two-time Heisman Trophy winner. He played
behind those big offensive lines at Ohio State and had a
lot of success, but he never panned out as a pro. When
you get to the NFL, it's a different game, a different level,
and his talents didn't blend in with what was needed.

I'm quite sure it bothered Archie to not have it pan out,
but he was just one example of how not everybody can
make it in pro ball no matter what kind of career he's had

in college. Yet Archie has gone on with his life, and he's doing quite well helping out with the football program at Ohio State.

Earl Campbell was one of the best runners I've ever seen for a big man. I consider him a modern-day Jim Brown. He had a few good years with Houston, but they wore him out. That man could run a football. He wasn't real fast, but he was fast enough. Big Earl would run over you and around you and could make you miss. I always like it when a runner makes a guy miss. The Houston Oilers sure got their money's worth out of Earl. They worked the heck out of him like some old plow horse. He took a lot of licks, a lot of hard licks. It's too bad that all that pounding eventually caught up to him.

Wilbert Montgomery was one of the toughest backs I ever saw. He was about my size, maybe even a little smaller than me. Wilbert had some great games for the Philadelphia Eagles, but the Cowboys used to love to play against him. A straight-ahead runner, not a physical guy, Wilbert took a lot of abuse because of his size. And he couldn't really punish many people even though he ran as if he could. Instead of running to daylight, Wilbert would run to contact. That was when the Cowboy defense liked to get its licks in. Wilbert's style of running and all the pounding he subjected his body to made his career short-lived. Man, the hits the guy took were unreal.

Among today's runners Eric Dickerson stands alone. Barring injury, he'll surpass all of us and rewrite the record books. Big, strong, flashy, elusive, Eric is blessed with God-given talent and an attitude to excel. He is a great player. But he's been fortunate to have played behind some of the best offensive lines of all time. I can't say he's the greatest running back ever, but he's up there. Yet I wonder what some of the other great running backs in

NFL history would have been able to do had they run behind the kind of offensive lines Eric has had.

Eric is a piece of work. He can run over people, but he can also cut back, stop, change direction. He's the kind of runner who has some moves, and fans can appreciate that. Eric is not like the bulldog type of runners, the guys who just run over people all the time and who become boring. They're kind of ugly to me.

My Denver team played against Indianapolis in 1988, and Eric had himself a game. He gained a lot of yards. I was on the sidelines watching one of his surges. "Man, did you see that hole they opened up for Eric?" I asked one of my teammates.

"What hole? That last hole he went through was no hole. It was a canyon."

But you've got to give the guy credit. He'll go through a hole or a canyon, turn a corner, follow his blocks, break some tackles, and go upfield.

I look at the guys Eric Dickerson plays behind. Those guys average nearly 300 pounds a man, and they're good, damn good. Shit, I could hide behind those guys. Nobody'd ever see me coming through the damn line.

Another running back that I admire is Marcus Allen of the L.A. Raiders. Marcus looks smaller than his 6'1", 205 pounds. But he doesn't wear a lot of pads. He's tough, tough as nails. I've seen him take some hard hits in his stride. A guy who doesn't work with a whole lot of offensive support, Marcus is an outstanding competitor. He's got quick feet, great vision, and real good hands.

One player who hasn't gotten the full glamour treatment as a running back is Roger Craig of the San Francisco 49ers. The players in the NFL respect him, and that's what counts. I think a lot of him. Roger is a strong, powerful runner. You like watching him because of his style. He looks like a big Clydesdale pumping up there with his high knee action and legs churning like pistons. It was nice to see him do so well in the Super Bowl against Cincinnati and get all that national recognition.

When you look at Bo Jackson of the Raiders, at 6'2", 240 pounds, he's an amazing physical specimen. Bo is the freak of freaks, and I say that in a positive way. To be that big, that strong, and that fast is something else. Bo is a guy who can run over a defender or make the defender miss him. That's the difference between Bo and Herschel Walker, whom I consider to be a bulldog type of runner. How good will Bo Jackson be? It's too early to tell. He comes in and plays, and then he doesn't play because of nagging injuries. He'll have to pass the test of time.

Joe Morris of the New York Giants had that one great year. But he hasn't really come back for his encore. Joe is small, but strong and capable. With him, as with a lot of other running backs, there is that one great season, and the next year they're all waiting to see what he can do. Will Joe Morris have a great career? Time will tell.

"Ironhead" Heyward came out of my alma mater, Pitt, and is a new guy in the league. I really don't know what to say about big Craig, a running back in a lineman's body. He's probably the biggest running back you'll ever see. Ironhead can run over people, and for a big guy, he can be pretty elusive. He can make people miss. I'd like to see him slim down. He can probably carry all that weight for a few years. But as he gets older, it'll prove to be a problem for him. I definitely think big Craig can be an outstanding back in the NFL.

Curt Warner of Seattle is one of the real tough runners in the league. It's amazing how he came back from that knee surgery he had a couple of years ago and still can play as well as he does on that AstroTurf up there in the Kingdome.

Lionel James is a great competitor with versatility.

That "Little Train" is more than just a runner—his being a great return man makes him an asset to any team. And Gary Anderson on the Chargers is a good back with quick feet. He's also an asset because of his versatility— Gary is a fine receiver.

Versatility in a running back is a great asset to any offense. Not too many backs catch the ball well—there's Herschel Walker, Marcus Allen. To do it year in and year out, you have to be thrown to on a consistent basis. I was never thrown to very much as a set part of my game. And I guess I've taken a nonchalant attitude toward pass receiving because my coaches never placed much emphasis on wanting me to do it.

Herschel Walker is one of the newest kids on the block, still in his infancy in the NFL. A semi-bulldog type, not very flashy, Herschel gets the job done. I'd like to see him develop more ability to make people miss. He's more of a power runner, a guy who goes straight ahead. Yet Herschel has the size, strength, speed, and attitude to be as great as anybody.

Today, I'm maybe the last back of my size to accomplish what I've accomplished. I don't know what it is— maybe guys are eating better foods or something—but they're all getting bigger, stronger, and faster.

When I first came into the NFL in 1977 at 185 pounds, people said I was too small to survive in this league. Now, after all these years, people look at the list of all-time great running backs. They see Walter Payton, then Tony Dorsett, and then Jim Brown and the others. To have my name in there in that company is really something.

I don't want to say what I have accomplished has surprised me. But I guess it has surprised a lot of people, many of the so-called football experts. I knew what my

abilities were. I knew the nature of the business, and
what I didn't know I made it my business to learn.

Dallas is my adopted city and I've seen it grow and
become more cosmopolitan, more tolerant, a different
kind of place. No doubt it is my favorite city, just as
Texas Stadium is my favorite stadium, and that's not just
because it was where I had so much glory.

It's simply a great facility. The playing field is excellent. There's a little crown on it, so it's not totally flat like
some of the places that are used for both baseball and
football.

Texas Stadium seats 65,101 and is a wonderful place
for fans to watch football. Everything about it is first-
class. There are a couple of hundred suites that seat a
dozen people each. They're decorated in all kinds of
styles, a couple like Arab palaces. Some of them have
mahogany bars, crystal chandeliers, butlers in tuxedos.
Even the enclosed press box is posh with upholstered
leather chairs and pretty cowgirls serving barbecued beef
and Texas chili.

What I don't like about Texas Stadium is the 2¼-acre
opening in the middle of the roof. I wish they'd totally
enclose it. But Clint Murchison liked the hole. He said he
didn't like watching football in the completely enclosed
Astrodome.

"We could have easily closed up the hole in the roof,"
he said. "But this way our fans are protected from the
weather and they can still see the sky." Well, maybe he
had a point.

The fans there are great fans, but they're also a certain
type. As a player you look behind the bench and you see
people coming out into the stands wearing mink coats,
dressed up in expensive suits, and this and that. You

wonder whether it's a fashion show, an Easter parade, or whether they've come to watch a sporting event.

It's a little like former Cowboy tight end Billy Truax said: "The whole place is weird. You're down there on the field and you know they're up there. It's like the lions and the Christians all over again. We'd better keep winning. Thumbs up is better than thumbs down."

For a lot of years it was thumbs up. The fans, and they love the Cowboys, would come in there and sit down and not cheer very loud. They became somewhat spoiled over the years because of all the success the Cowboys had. But I always felt they should have been more boisterous. When you talk about the intangibles, the twelfth man, I believe that fans can really play a role in inspiring a team to play well. As a player, if you feel all the electricity that can be generated in a stadium—it inspires you, pumps you up. Now that the Cowboys are losing, the fans are making noise, much more noise, in Texas Stadium, but a lot of it is boos. It's thumbs down instead of all of those years of thumbs up.

New Orleans is another favorite place for me. Winning the national championship there while playing for Pitt, then winning the Super Bowl there with the Cowboys, developed in me a true liking for the city. It has good memories for me. I like the people there, the food, the atmosphere. I even like the Superdome, as big and humongous a place as it is.

I've played in just about every stadium there is in the National Football League—except one of the fields in Green Bay and at Tampa Bay. Three Rivers Stadium is a place I've played in as a collegian and also as a pro. I don't like it too much. There's something about the surfaces that are used for both baseball and football that bother me.

I do like the Coliseum in Los Angeles. It's a big old

place with a lot of history and tradition to it. Although
the fans are far away and you don't feel the intimacy that
you can feel in other stadiums, it's a unique place for
football.

The domed stadiums in Seattle, Minnesota, and New
Orleans always present challenges for me coming in as a
visiting player. They're tough places for a visiting team.
All the noise those fans make has no place to escape. A
team that has a domed stadium always has an edge. If
you come in there and find yourself backed up in a short-
yardage situation, the crowd can really get into it and
take over. But if you can come in as the visiting team and
score early, it shows the crowd that you've invaded their
territory. It puts a silencer on those people. As an athlete
you enjoy the challenge of the domed stadiums and the
challenge of taking the crowd out of the game. Silencing
the home crowd is a real thrill.

I'm not a big fan of the artificial surface—I wish they'd
go back to grass. The artificial surface is rough and sub-
jects your body to a lot of wear and tear. I'm sure that if
all the games were played on natural grass, careers
would last longer and there would be fewer injuries. I
never liked playing in St. Louis for that reason, because
of the artificial turf.

The artificial surface is antiseptic. On grass you get
that old-time look for every game—dirt, a soiled uniform,
a little blood here and there mixed in with the elements,
like in the old days, the old mud games.

I've played on all kinds of fields in all kinds of weather
—downpours, fog, sleet, freezing cold weather. Fortunately, I never had to play in snow. But playing on a nice
sunny day, when the outcome of a game does not depend
on the elements, is what I like best.

I think that games played in subzero temperatures are
ridiculous. Guys try to block the cold out of their minds,

but I feel very strongly that playing in those conditions does not make for a real competitive football game. What with the time-outs and delays in a game, players are out there freezing their butts off. The ball is so cold that it's being dropped because guys can't hold on to it. Playing in those arctic conditions is not fair to the fans and it's also not fair to the teams. The outcome of a game should not be determined by the weather; it should be a result of how teams play the game.

But there's not much you can do about it all except postpone the game or require domed stadiums in cities where the weather gets that bad. People defend those kinds of games saying they're part of the character of football, seeing all those guys bundled up, shivering, steam coming out of their mouths. To me it makes for good film highlights but for poor football.

Realizing all through my career how tough it is out there on the football field, I consider myself very fortunate to have avoided any real violence, any real pounding. I've been blessed with the ability to get my arms, head, and neck out of the way and not get hit as often as a lot of other runners. I've also taken special precautions.

A lot of players dress to be in style, to look good on TV. They have their socks pulled up, their uniforms are tailored and tight-fitting, they have some of this, some of that showing. I was never like that. I would always dress like I was going to work—fully padded.

"Man, you look kind of chubby," some guys would comment. "You look like a roly-poly with all that padding."

"I'm not dressing for image like you are," I would tell them. "I'm not all prettied up for TV. When I get the ball people are going to try and hit me from every direction possible. I don't care about looking good in my uniform. I care about covering up every part of me that I can cover up. I care about protecting myself."

To this day I still get teased about the way I have pads all over me. I guess, along with Eric Dickerson, I'm one of the more padded backs in the league. But I don't see anything wrong with that.

The padding dates all the way back to my high school times, and there's no way I'll play in a game without that stuff on my body. Knock on wood, all that padding has been good for me. I've never had a hip pointer or any nagging problems from a hit.

The thigh pads that I wear are much bigger than most. I also wear pretty long knee pads. At one time when I had cracked ribs, I was wearing even bigger rib pads than I do now.

At one time I also started wearing a shaded Plexiglas shield. Every year, it seemed, I would have experiences with someone sticking his fingers in my eye, or on my cutbacks hands would whack me around the eyes. There was a time when I had developed an irritation in my eyes and couldn't stand the sunlight. That's when I decided to put on the shield.

I wore it for a while and kind of liked it. If I wanted to cheat and look in the direction that I was going to run— defenders couldn't see my eyes behind the shield.

Then one day we were getting set to play a game in Kansas City. During the pre-game warm-up it was pouring down rain. I had to keep wiping away at that shield to be able to see. It was a pain. I told them to take off the shield. I've never used it again. But although I did away with the shield, I'll never take off the padding.

With all the padding, with my ability to hello-and-goodbye defenders, with my knack of pulling my head and limbs out of harm's way, I've still experienced my share of pain.

In a game in Philadelphia, I was stood up and really run over. I felt it coming, but there was nothing I could do about it. I was hung out to dry. Dennis Harrison put his helmet right in my ribs and I felt it immediately. But I kept trying to tough it out.

As the game moved on I was getting hit after that and I would be grunting and moaning, "Ohh. Ohh."

Guys would come over to me. They were concerned. "Are you okay?"

"Yeah, yeah," I told them. I didn't want them reminding me of how bad I felt.

But the pain was unbearable. I was moaning and groaning so much out there on the field that even the defensive linemen, the guys we were playing against, became worried.

"Is he all right?" they were asking my teammates. "Get him out of here," they were telling guys on the Cowboys. I had the feeling that every time I got hit, people were taking bets on whether I'd get up or not. I felt like my bell was rung, like a dishrag doll.

But I didn't want to leave the game. In regular life I would bump my hand or finger and I would feel it and make a big deal out of it. In football I had conditioned myself to endure pain. I was getting paid to play and I was supposed to pay with pain—that was my way of thinking.

Finally, my teammates got a hold of me and just pushed me back to the bench. "You're out of there," they said. "You can't play any more." They were right.

In my early years with Dallas, in a game against St. Louis, I was running down the left sideline toward the Cardinals' bench. One of their big lineman was pursuing me—I saw him coming but there was nothing I could do but take the blow. All I saw was this big old arm come out. Pow! I was hit straight across the head. Like a shot, I

went straight down to the turf. I was knocked out for a
few moments. Man, my lights were out. But I came to
pretty fast.

"You okay?" Jay Saldi was one of the first guys on our
team to get over to me. "You okay, Tony?"

"Man, this guy just nearly took my head off and you're
asking me if I'm okay." I wondered if Jay was okay.

Back in the huddle I kept telling Roger Staubach,
"Don't run me again, Roger, I can't run now."

I knew I'd be okay after a while, but for a few moments
I wasn't totally there. That was probably one of the hard-
est hits I ever got and I still shudder a bit when I think of
that forearm smashing into my head. It was an ugly, uncalled-for shot.

Overall, I was lucky to avoid crippling injuries. Football in the NFL is very physical and violent. But it's violent within the rules. It's a rough game, and guys want to
play well and look good out there. But today, if there's a
chance for a guy to really ruin someone, lots of players
will pull up and pull away.

On any given day you can pick up a newspaper or listen to a sports show and there's a big deal being made
out of all the injuries to quarterbacks. Some people claim
that the reason for quarterback injuries is that guys are
out there intentionally trying to knock the hell out of
them.

But that's not the reason. A quarterback's body is just
not conditioned to take the pounding the rest of us take.
In practice, teams will not allow their quarterbacks to get
hit—they blow the whistle. Everyone knows what a valuable commodity a quarterback is and that he can make or
break a team's season. So teams just don't allow a quarterback to take any unnecessary abuse. But since the
quarterback is not used to getting hit, since his body is
not conditioned to that kind of thing, when he does take a

hit his body does not respond to the pain and injury the way other players do.

Brian Bosworth had a lot of negative things to say about the NFL refs in his book—that they blow calls, that they're out of shape, that they get in the way of players. I've been around the league and around the refs much longer than the Boz has, and I disagree with him. I think NFL refs do one hell of a job, game after game, considering it's almost impossible for them to see everything out there. Sure, they make mistakes because sometimes they don't have the right angle or they can be intimidated by the crowd. But they're not robots or machines. They're not up there in the press box where they can see everything with the instant replay at their side.

As for their conditioning, their being in shape—I'm not worried about that. I've seen players in the NFL with ugly bodies—some of those guys are hardly in the best of shape. What do the NFL refs have to be in such great shape for? They're not sprinting anywhere. All you want is for them to have good vision and clear judgment.

I've always tried to avoid running into a ref, but I've banged into one or two of them in my time. Some players have mowed down refs like bowling pins—those have been pretty bad hits, especially since the refs don't have any padding to cushion the blows.

There's still some controversy about the instant replay being used in games. I've been in favor of it from the start because you hate to see an important ball game decided by a bad call. If they can go up top and replay the play and reverse the call because of something that was missed, that makes instant replay a great addition to football.

Throughout my career I have always been sensitive to racial matters, but they have never consumed me. I have never been a prejudiced person. Sure, back in Aliquippa during my early years we had some little racial scuffles. I participated in them, but I never had any serious hang-ups about black, white, or any other race. I was never a Black Power advocate, a guy who walked around with my fist balled up.

There has been stuff written about me that I know had a racial tinge. It was like, being black, I was a more visible, more open target for the poison pens. I hated it.

Through the years I've gotten together with Jesse Jackson to talk and share experiences. He's had a strong influence on me in dealing with the media. Jesse told me about writers misquoting him, tearing him apart, slanting stories against him.

"You fall right into the media's hands if you get angry, if you don't talk to them," he said. "The best way, Tony, is to do the exact opposite of what they expect you to do. And especially don't let them see they've gotten to you."

I'm no Jesse Jackson—far from it. But I've tried to follow his advice and it's helped me a lot.

In Dallas, I was a controversial guy. Yet if I had been white or even a good old boy, maybe it would've been a lot different for me. Maybe I would've been left alone to do my own thing. Maybe I could have had Dallas in the palm of my hand.

I'm not knocking Dallas, because I've always realized that it's a city in the Deep South, a southern city with its own mentality. I've even seen the city grow quite a bit and become more tolerant through the years. So there's been some progress on that scene. I realize, too, that prejudice exists everywhere. It's just that maybe it's there in Dallas a little more than in other places.

There have always been plenty of black players on the

Cowboys, but a lot of them have come out of Dallas with
nothing, have retired without the dignity of a lot of the
white players. It seems management doesn't help the
black guys once their careers are over as much as they
help the white players. I've talked with a lot of former
black Cowboys. "Man, it's tough for us to do something
out here," they say. They came back to the franchise asking for help in setting up a business or some such and
they couldn't get anything.

Yet John Niland was a guy who every other week, it
seemed, was having some problems: drugs, forgery, bum
checks, whatever. I don't know whether it was because
Niland was a white ex-player, but you'd always see
somebody in the Cowboys' front office defending him,
helping him out. That kind of double standard is not right.
It's somewhat shocking, but I know that that's the way of
the society.

Jimmy the Greek got himself into a lot of hot water and
lost his job with his comments about race and the black
athlete. I always liked Jimmy and my experiences with
him were always very positive. He was a guy who liked
the center of the stage.

Jimmy said some stuff about the black man and the
black woman being bred for physical things and having
better natural athletic ability because of bigger muscles
and being faster. I agree with that. Jim Kelly, the Buffalo
quarterback, also seems to agree with that.

In a game last season Kelly's read was to throw to one
receiver. But he threw to another guy. "I saw this white
guy out there covering our black receiver," Kelly explained later. "And I knew there was no way the white
guy could stay with him, so I threw the ball and got the
touchdown."

Kelly got the touchdown, but Jimmy the Greek Snyder
got the boot when he went on to talk about blacks in

football, saying, "What else do you people want? If you become black coaches, you'll have it all."

Maybe Jimmy shouldn't have said what he said, or maybe he should have said it in a different way. But what he said is what a lot of people think. Knowing Jimmy, I don't believe he thought he was making a racial slur. Even if he did think that way, it was not the kind of thing a guy like him would say in public and especially not on camera.

More than anything else, the timing of what Jimmy said cost him his job. The NFL is trying to get more black coaches, more black quarterbacks. His statements on such a touchy issue made him something of a scapegoat.

The NFL has never had a black head coach. Of course, there are tons of assistants—that keeps up the quota. But there's no way any one can prove to me that there isn't one black guy qualified to be a head coach. Yet no team seems to have the courage to be the first one to bring him in.

For that matter, there are very few black quarterbacks in the NFL. Although there are plenty of them in college football, in the pros you can count the guys on the fingers of one hand. Dallas doesn't have a black quarterback, and I don't see the Cowboys ever having a black quarterback starting for them.

Although there are just three black starting quarterbacks in the league now, they're sure not there because of any tokenism. They're there because they can play the game. And I think an awful lot of them.

Warren Moon is a tremendous passer and some kind of scrambler. Very astute and a great athlete, Warren finally got his just due when he was selected for the Pro Bowl last season.

I started to develop some admiration for Doug Williams when he was in Tampa Bay playing for a terrible team. Ed "Too Tall" Jones would be coming up and be draped all over him and Doug would still be throwing the ball. He's extremely strong.

We'd be there watching him. "Man," some guy would say, "why doesn't that Williams just get down or throw the ball away and quit taking all that abuse?" There was never any quit in him. Doug would always be in there standing strong. And he'd use that rifle arm of his to throw the heck out of the football.

I was glad to see Doug have the great Super Bowl with Washington a couple of years ago. Last season he was hurt and didn't have a good year. But with Washington, he has the offensive line in front of him and the receivers to throw to that will make people forget about last year. He'll come back.

Randall Cunningham is another black quarterback that I like a lot. He's coming into his own on the Eagles. Some people might think he's a little cocky, but I think a lot of that is confidence, not cockiness. Randall's done some phenomenal things; he's a super athlete and is capable of becoming one of the top quarterbacks in the league.

Professional football is a great game. It's a great sport and a great life. But what it's all about is big business. Anybody who is involved with it in any way and feels any differently is just fooling himself.

The NFL is a high-pressure business—cash is the bottom line. The revenues generated through ticket sales, television, and pay TV are astronomical. Now the NFL's even branching out into foreign countries.

The one expendable commodity in the sport is the players. There's going to come a time, whether it's through age or injury, when a guy finds himself out of this business. That's part of the deal.

But also part of the deal is a lot of inhumane treatment.

And there's so much of it. I can't understand how one
human being can treat another human being the way I've
seen myself and others treated. There's a lot of meanness. From that standpoint it's tough, and that's one of
the reasons why I would never want to push my son into
playing professional football.

Sure, there's a lot of glory, glamour and financial re-
wards. I've had all of that. But there are a lot of mental
things that players go through, all the pressures, all the
demands. Some of those things have collapsed a person
or destroyed a life.

I have thought many times about the old expression
"meat on the hoof." That's all players are in many cases
—pieces of meat getting abused and misused. Lots of
players come out of football, after giving so many years
to the game, with nothing to show for it. And they've
abused their bodies, played with pain and pressure,
played with reckless abandon, played with the chance of
losing their lives or being paralyzed for life.

It's very sad for me to hear the leader of our Players'
Association, Gene Upshaw, tell us that the owners don't
want to determine or investigate why a large percentage
of professional football players die at a very young age.
Maybe the owners would do something if they knew, but
the fact that they don't want to know is very shocking to
me.

Professional football is such a closed-in big business
that a battle was waged for years to get free agency for
the players. I had thought that the owners, who are so
tight with each other and cooperate and fraternize so
much, would never let free agency happen. Now there is
free agency in the NFL. But will anything come of it?

Last year I was feeling a bit sorry for Tom Landry, the
way the media were on him and all that. The way they
were trying to run him out of town was sad. I was think-

ing, sure, he's had a losing season, but it's not all his fault.

Then I heard about how the Dallas Cowboys released my buddy Mike Hegman, a guy out of Tennessee State, a guy who had been giving up his body for them for thirteen years. They cut him at mid-season.

That's what I hate most of all about football. Guys who have been around so long start slipping a little, and management just drops them like a hot potato. They go on to the next man. We'll use him up a while, and then we'll shit on him too. I think that's shitty.

I knew that Dallas owner Bum Bright's reasoning with Mike was that he was a guy on injured reserve, so why not save some money and get rid of him?

But Mike, in my opinion, is a better player than several of the younger guys they've got playing there in Dallas. I started thinking all kinds of things. I thought that if Mike were white they probably wouldn't have done that to him. I thought about how they had some guys on that team who shouldn't have even passed the physical.

My feeling sorry for the way Tom Landry was treated in the media then got lost in the perspective of how Tom and Dallas management treated Mike Hegman. They handled him like a piece of meat that they just cut away.

I've had no contact with any of the people who ran the Cowboys since I left the team, except for a Mailgram from Tom Landry when I passed Jim Brown on the all-time rushing list. I don't expect to hear from those people. Once you leave the Cowboys, unless you're Roger Staubach or someone like that, they don't have much to do with you. They have a business to run and lives of their own and that's all right with me.

If I see any of them, it'll probably be just like any other time. We'll say a few words to each other and be on our

ways. I don't have any hard feelings toward them. I hope
they don't have any toward me. If they do, then they do.

I still consider Tom Landry the best football mind
around. You had to respect the man as far as preparing a
team for a game was concerned. He covered everything.
Tom had such a feel for the game that he could predict
what would happen out on the field all the time.

With the Dallas Cowboys on a downslide there were
all of these attacks on Tom Landry and what he'd done
with the team. I still think he's a great coach. His record
speaks for itself—all the things he's accomplished. But in
the center of his ways he hadn't changed in years. If he
had changed it would have helped the Cowboys.

When everybody else is changing, you have to change
too if you want to still be up with the best. You have to
change, go with the flow, or else you get lost in the shuf-
fle.

When Buddy Ryan was with Chicago and brought in
what he called the Bear defense—that was a change. Everybody's been changing throughout the league. But you
haven't seen Dallas changing that much. All over the NFL
teams started developing big offensive lines. The Cowboys, previously the innovators, in this case were the fol-
lowers. It took the Cowboys and Tom Landry a few years
before they started to do what others had already done.

People asked, "What had Tom Landry brought to football lately?" Sure, years back he brought in the multiple
offense, the shotgun, and back in my rookie year he
would put a back or a tight end in motion and trap a man
over center. That was a good innovation and worked
well. But when people asked what Tom Landry had done
lately, it was a legitimate question.

Tom was still using the flex defense. That was his
thing. Of course, it can be quite successful if you've got

the right people out there because it shuts down the lanes against the run.

But I don't like the flex. A lot of players don't like it. But that was Tom—staying with something that was somewhat outdated. Nobody in the National Football League uses it anymore. So that should tell you something about it.

The first reaction in the flex is to read. Doing that takes away aggression. It's read and then react. In my opinion defense has to be played with a reckless abandon. It shouldn't be guys catching a block, reading, then doing something about what they see. I believe in letting it all hang out. I believe in aggression out there.

Every time I would see Ed "Too Tall" Jones down on the field in a four-point stance, it was like I was looking at a frog, a giant frog. Keeping Ed in the flex cut him off from all he could be. Ed is one of the most underrated defensive ends I've ever seen. Playing on the strong side of the flex defense for Dallas, he does a hell of a job. But he's there in a controlled defense, a controlled situation. I always thought that Ed could have been up there among the sack leaders, that he could have been a perennial Pro Bowler, if Dallas had played a regular 4-3 or 3-4, whatever. If Tom had just turned him and Randy White loose, that would have been something.

The Dallas system, and I guess what we're talking about here was the Tom Landry system, did not enhance the ability of players—it took away from it in many instances.

There were guys that I saw come into Dallas, young guys who had been great athletes in college, and they would be made to fit into that Dallas defense. Thinking, not reacting, they were not able to show their natural ability. The system, not their instincts, determined what

they did. And that's not how you get the most out of
football players.

There's a parallel in all that with the way I was treated
when I first got to Dallas. Coaches would be breaking
down things for me, putting me in a kind of lockstep,
giving me directions on how to run.

I would get into shouting matches with them. "Do it our
way, Tony," they would tell me.

"No," I would respond. "I'm gonna do it my way. Don't
try and make a robot out of me."

I knew that running by the numbers was not me. My
spontaneity is me. My creativeness is me. I realized almost at the very start of my career that I couldn't satisfy
them. I had to satisfy me.

Maybe I was unique in that I challenged them, I fought
to be my own person, because throughout the years I'd
see players come into Dallas and they'd go along with
whatever the coaches told them to do. That was nice, but
it also cut many guys off from what got them there in the
first place—their natural talent. So there was a flaw built
into the system. It all goes back to that old Shakespeare
expression about the fault not being in our stars but in
ourselves.

A football team can't stay on top all the time, but it
doesn't have to suffer such a drastic turnaround as Dallas
has over the past couple of years.

When players are cut off from their talent, when the
talent is not there, when a coach, no matter how great, is
stuck in his ways—you can't overcome things like that.
And that's all part of the reason for the decline and fall of
the Dallas Cowboys.

When I first came into the profession of pro football, I
realized that I couldn't survive by overpowering people.
That was not my way in college, and it hasn't been my
way in the National Football League. If I played at

6'2" and 225 pounds, it might be possible for me to get by on power, but at 5'11" and playing most of the time at 183 pounds, I've always tried to slip and slide, to hello-and-goodbye you. I'm always trying to negotiate, to maneuver, to move away from the contact. But unlike some other guys who gained big reputations in the NFL, I will take a hit if I have to and not hide and run the ball out of bounds.

When I run I sometimes think I see too much, and that can even work against me. I see the colors of the opposition, lots of blips of light, beams that might be the colors off their uniforms. Over the years all of that has steered me through trouble.

For example, once in St. Louis during one of my early years in the league the ball was on the Cardinals' four-yard line. It was a play off left tackle at high speed. The right defensive end came crashing down to get me; the right linebacker was filling it up and the two corners were on a blitz.

Somehow, some way, even though I was moving out at full steam, I felt all these people converging on me. I pivoted on my right foot, stepped straight back out of the hole, did a 360. Roger Wehrli and Carl Allen, the corners, collided head-on in the place where I had been a split second before. I spun out wide around the left end. The safety seemed to have me hemmed in, but I turned it on and outran him into the end zone for a touchdown.

Lots of times I've gotten out of situations just like that but not in the same way. On that play, I don't know what I saw. I knew people were coming, and I stepped back into a spin, and then something took me over and got me out of there and into the end zone. It was incredible. Looking at game films, I know that there's someone else other than me making things happen. It was like an outside force was taking control of what I was doing.

To this day I watch films to pick up tendencies and characteristics of defensive players. But, overall, running is instinct, knowing my blocking schemes, getting a feel for where there may be some softness. It's all reaction. For me it's going to the point of attack and then it's improvising.

Basically, runners don't pattern themselves after other runners. Although I saw a lot of O. J. Simpson in Marcus Allen early in his career, I don't know if that was a conscious thing with Marcus or not. I know I wasn't influenced by anybody except maybe my brothers. My style is just my style. It was something I was born with.

You can draw all the X's and O's and diagram plays, but sometimes runners have to follow their instincts. I was probably the first guy to do a 360 spin on a regular basis. Robert Newhouse would tell me I was crazy for doing that, but it was something that came naturally. I'd catch the guys coming at me, and then at full speed—boom!—I'd go into a spinning circular move, and I'd be gone. It was like break dancing in a football uniform. After a time there were a few more players doing it, and then a lot of them picked up the move.

When I got to Denver, Dan Reeves and I reminisced about one of my rookie running experiences with Dallas when he was one of the assistant coaches. We had a play called "Slant 24." And in the practices, Dan always told me I ran the play the wrong way. What I would do was see some softness in the defense and run away from people. I gained lots of yardage rolling the play all the way back from the defenders.

"That was a good run," Dan had said. "But it'll never happen that way in a game."

"We'll see." I smiled.

In a game against St. Louis, Terry Metcalf had scored a 70-yard-plus touchdown against us. On our next series I ran about 77 yards for a touchdown on "Slant 24" exactly the way Dan said it would never happen.

"What are you trying to do, Tony, show me up?" Dan kidded me as I got to the sidelines. "I told you that play would never happen that way."

"Well, Dan," I kidded him back, "I guess it shows a runner just has to be a runner."

E P I L O G U E

TO SUCCEED IN THE NFL AND, I GUESS, IN LIFE, YOU need to find something to hold on to, something to motivate you, something to inspire you. There were always people saying that I couldn't do it, that I was too small, that I couldn't do this, that I couldn't do that. Those were big tools for me. They pushed me. They drove me to prove those people wrong.

I've been lucky. I thank God for that. It's tough as hell out there on the football field and it gets tougher as you get older. What I've accomplished in football has come from a combination of God-given talent and intestinal fortitude. No doubt, I also couldn't have accomplished anything by myself. All the people I've come into contact with who encouraged me—the fans, the coaches, my teammates, even opposing players—all of them contributed to my success.

Making big money never really crossed my mind. I was always thinking about being the best at what I did. All the other stuff: the fame, the respect, the recognition, the awards, and the money . . . I knew those things would all come along if I did my best.

It's been a long and exciting experience for me. I've met so many people in so many cities and towns, been all over the United States. I've been to the White House, met Presidents Ford and Carter. I've met so many great people from all walks of life. Those are memories I cherish.

I think I've had a great career, a career most people would be more than happy to have had. As I look back now, there are only a few regrets.

I would have liked to run the ball more than I did. That's one regret. I cried out in Dallas for them to let me get my hands on the ball more. It didn't happen.

Another regret I have is maybe about some of the

things I said and did. I was young and full of fire and some of the things I said could have been said more diplomatically. But that was my personality and people expected that. I'm not saying I should have been that way because people expected it. But that was me. And I guess if I had to do it all over again, I probably would do most of the same things and say most of the same things, but not all of them.

I ran into people who were crazies, who would bump into me in my early years in pro football. Some would call me names or call me out. Sometimes I fought back.

I ran into groupies and took advantage of that situation. It was fun. But after a time all of that gets old. Today I hear guys talking about this woman, that woman, doing this with her, that with her. Now I find that quite humorous. I wonder if I was like that. I guess I was pretty much the same way back then. It was my ego doing the talking.

Another one of the regrets, a void in my life, is that I spend very little time going to church. I want to correct that. My brother-in-law is a preacher. My sister is very religious. My mom is a religious woman. So I come from a somewhat religious background.

Today a lot of hypocritical things in religion are becoming public knowledge. I saw a lot of that taking place in my early life. I feel very strongly that I don't have to pay for religion. If I want to go to church—I go. I hear a good sermon and feel good about myself and about the day and about whatever was said to me.

But I don't like that passing the plate around and being asked to give this amount or that amount of money. If I want to give—that's my business. I understand preachers get their money from offerings and dues and all that. But I just can't stand people wanting money for religion all the time.

I have religious beliefs, and I'm quite sure that some-

day I'll become a better Christian. People say to me that
the time is now, that you never know when your life is
going to be snatched from you. I'm not ready, not just yet,
to make that commitment.

From time to time I think about how a little kid from
Aliquippa, Pennsylvania, has been able to do the things
I've done, to make the kind of money I've made, to live
the lifestyle I've lived. People talk about the American
dream and I've truly lived that dream. In no place but
America could something like this happen to a person.
I'm not a political person, but I am patriotic. I love being
an American, seeing America.

I'm looking forward to playing one more year. I would
like to be on a winning team and be in the playoffs once
again. I would like to feel that I'm contributing to the
team's success, I would like to be used. Then, because of
the kind of athlete I've been, I would like to go out in
style, with some glory and some flair. But most important
of all is to help the Broncos win, to contribute to their
success. And after that, I'll be looking forward to some
new horizons.

I have always said that I wanted to leave this game of
football as I came into it—all in one piece and healthy.
God willing, I hope to survive that way. But the game is
so competitive that regardless of who you are they go
after you out there on the field. Guys might help me up a
little more than they used to, or compliment me on certain cuts or moves I make, maybe out of respect for my
ability, my longevity, and my accomplishments. Yet they
go after me the way they went after Kareem Abdul-Jabbar in his final season in the NBA last year at age forty-
one. He had such a brilliant career and impact on the
game of basketball that there were guys who felt that
they had accomplished something if they could block his
shot or hold him scoreless or to a low point total even

though he was in the twilight of his career. I guess they thought they would be able to brag to their children and grandchildren that they stopped a legend.

It's been the same way with me. In this business there's no one going out of his way to avoid getting a good lick on me. No matter how old you are or who you are, there's no kid gloves out there.

Most people respect what I've been able to accomplish over the years, especially when they realize what it's taken for a guy of my size to survive in the NFL for more than a decade. Most people think I'm a bigger person than I am.

I'd like to be remembered as an athlete who stepped out there between those white lines and gave 100 percent all the time. I'd also like to be remembered as a guy who gave the fans their money's worth every time they came out to see him play. Because whether I gained one yard or 99 yards, in that effort was all of me, all I had.

What I've come to realize about myself is that I was something of a maverick, a guy who didn't fit the system he played in, who couldn't be made into a clone and formed to fit the image. I have no regrets about that, because I see that being me was a major part of my success.

My story is like that of a spirited colt who runs as he wants to, who runs free. The colt has all the verve and energy in the world until someone comes along and puts a rope, bridle, and saddle on him. Then he becomes a lot like all the other horses.

I always tried to keep a lot of the wild colt in me. I always knew that losing or giving up my individuality might have made somebody else happy. But it would have been no good for Tony Dorsett. It would have hurt me as an athlete; it would have hurt me as a person.

Running my way was the way it had to be. Running tough.

AS THIS BOOK WAS GOING INTO THE FINAL
stages of editing, the Dallas Cowboys were sold. With
new ownership coming in, I don't think it was a surprise
to anyone that Tom Landry was no longer going to be
coaching the team. But the way Landry's release was
handled left a lot of people unhappy.

Tom Landry had been in Dallas for twenty-nine years
and was one of the most visible personalities in the National Football League. He was almost like a permanent
fixture. At least we thought he was. It seemed to everyone that Tom would never be fired, would never be dealt
with the way he was. But I guess his dismissal just goes
to show that *no one* is really secure in this business.
Those are just the hard and cold facts about it. Anyone
can be fired.

I've seen a lot of players treated the way Tom was—
without any forewarning, without any respect. But you
just felt that would never happen to Tom because he was
a class guy who meant so much to the National Football
League for so many years. But it happened. He did it to a
lot of players over the years, and now it's happened to
him.

When you think about the whole scenario, instead of
the new owner, Jerry Jones, saying "I'm here and Jimmy
Johnson is here," it might have been better if he had said,
"I'm the new owner now, and I've decided to make some
changes and start over and bring in some new young
ideas and a guy I believe can change things."

But Jerry Jones was caught up in all the emotions—the
emotions of buying a professional football franchise and
having his good friend Jimmy Johnson as a coach. He
didn't have the time, I guess, to handle the situation a
little better.

There's no doubt in my mind that Tom and Alicia Landry will be just fine. This first year away from the team will be the toughest—watching the Cowboys, seeing the Cowboys coached by someone else. It's going to be strange, too, for the people in Dallas, not seeing the man wearing the hat walking up and down the sidelines at Texas Stadium.

But I think the Dallas fans just have to have an open mind and accept the change. It was going to happen eventually, anyway. The fans should give Jerry Jones and Jimmy Johnson all the support they can. The new management will need the help of the Dallas community to make the team a success.

Personally I thought the whole deal with Tom Landry could have been handled better. But, as some people say, "What goes around, comes around." You hate to think of that when you're thinking of Tom Landry. But, in reality, that's basically what it boils down to.

I wish Tom nothing but the best. I had my disputes and misunderstandings with him, but I've always admired him. Mrs. Landry, too, is a very classy lady, and one of the few people who understood Tom.

I felt for Tom Landry, the way things ended, and I hope one day our paths will cross again.

Harvey Frommer is a sports historian and journalist. The author of more than twenty-six books and five hundred articles, he most recently wrote *Red on Red: The Autobiography of Red Holzman* and *Throwing Heat: The Autobiography of Nolan Ryan*.